Business Success Through Service Excellence

Business Success Through Service Excellence

Moira Clark and Susan Baker

ELSEVIER
BUTTERWORTH
HEINEMANN

Amsterdam • Boston • Heidelberg • London • New York • Oxford
Paris • San Diego • San Francisco • Singapore • Sydney • Tokyo

Elsevier Butterworth-Heinemann
Linacre House, Jordan Hill, Oxford OX2 8DP
200 Wheeler Road, Burlington, MA 01803

First published 2004

British Library Cataloguing in Publication Data
A catalogue record for this book is available from the British Library

Library of Congress Cataloguing in Publication Data
A catalogue record for this book is available from the Library of Congress

ISBN 0 7506 6085 6

For information on all Elsevier Butterworth-Heinemann publications
visit our website at http://books.elsevier.com

Typeset by Charon Tec Pvt Ltd, Chennai, India
Printed and bound in Great Britain by
Biddles Ltd, Kings Lynn, Norfolk

Contents

List of figures

List of tables

Foreword

We are all conditioned by experience.

We know it from the works of Darwin, Pavlov, Skinner and a whole host more. It is even woven into the fabric of our everyday speech:

You'll learn from (and with) experience!
Experience has taught me. . . .
The experience I gained has enabled me to. . . .

Not only is experience the basis for our survival, it is also our springboard for growth.

Yet why then, if we know this at the personal level, do businesses find it so difficult to incorporate this concept into the way they function?

Why do organisations still focus on customer satisfaction? It is, after all the lowest acceptable level of service and no indicator of future customer trends.

Why do they perform the same old surveys? Many of which are not acted upon and even fewer reward the customer with direct feedback or even thanks.

And why is the concept of customer service normally only discussed with a relatively small proportion of the company?

Leading organisations are working differently. They have learned and understood some basic concepts and then diligently and passionately executed against them with enthusiastic support from their employees.

So, what are some of the basics?

First, they know that the primary differentiator in today's market-place is the customer experience and neither the product (regardless of whether it is an airline seat, a current account or a visit to the vet) and nor, indeed, the price. And, by the way, I am referring to the total experience, not just the experience at the point of sale or initial contact.

Secondly, they know that to enhance the customer experience they need to have happy, positive, motivated and passionate employees who are knowledgeable and empathetic.

Thirdly, they know that customers do not stop spending money but in the absence of service excellence,they might just stop spending it with them.

Against this backdrop they know they need to focus on two key attributes, namely customer loyalty and customer advocacy, and they centre all of their activities on strengthening these areas. They know that loyal customers will return time after time and continue to invest in their business, and they know that their advocates will become their ultimate marketing weapon: telling others the good news.

So how do they go about this? What sets them apart?

First, they have a vision, something that both employees and customers can relate to and understand. It is not a complex statement of values or metrics, but it does need to portray a message and promote an emotional response. It can be as simple as 'To create customer experiences which inspire recommendation.' This does not talk about being the biggest or the best. It does not even say how to achieve the goal, but everyone understands the goal and their obligation to perform against it.

Leading organisations are also good listening organisations. They are in touch not only with their current customers but also their potential customers. Many create, in one form or other, 'The voice of the customer.' They create listening posts that help them understand the competitive marketplace and guide their future actions.

They understand the necessity and benefit of end-to-end involvement and participation within their organisation. They understand that good ideas can, and do, come from anywhere, not just senior management.

They understand great leadership is about identifying goals, explaining why they are important and helping others understand how to achieve them. It is about employee participation, motivation and involvement, not command and control. It is also about openness and creativity not restrictions and limitations.

Excellent organisations also understand that principles are more powerful than policies and, therefore, arm their employees with a few guiding principles which can assist the employee in any difficult situation. Again, keeping it simple is better: 'Make a promise keep a promise' or 'Do the right thing.' These articulations of principles are simple, effective and consistently promote the right kind of behaviours that enhance the customer experience.

Based upon hundreds of examples of best practice in the area of customer interaction, this book can guide you and your organisation on how to listen more attentively; create a vision for the future; involve and motivate your employees; measure your success, and, hopefully, drive you to market leadership.

Read, learn, apply and enjoy.

Brian H. Hadfield
Managing Director
Unisys

Acknowledgements

We have been involved in the Service Excellence Awards for the past seven years and during that time have continued to be inspired by the calibre of the entrants and the stories they have to tell. In bringing these narratives together in this book, we would like to acknowledge the contributions of a number of individuals and companies. Many people have helped to make it happen, but we would particularly like to thank Barry Townsend, Vice President of Customer-Focused Business Excellence at Unisys, for his unfailing support and encouragement. We also owe a debt of gratitude to Tony Locke, Service Excellence Awards Programme Manager. Tony is known to all the entrants as the person who orchestrates the Service Excellence Awards process and without his help in pulling together the source material, this book would not have been possible.

We must also thank Paul May who tirelessly worked with us in the preparation of the majority of the case studies featured in the following chapters. Additional thanks go to Alex Garrett who has not only worked as a journalist in the preparation of the Management Today supplement, but has also been instrumental in the creation of one of the cases included in the book.

The judging process has been a source of great pleasure to us over the years. It has been particularly delightful to work with a group of individuals, all dedicated to the pursuit of service excellence and who have consistently taken the judging seriously, ensuring that the professional standards of the Awards have been upheld and maintained.

We would also like to show our appreciation to all the organisations that have entered the Awards. Nearly one thousand companies have taken part since the programme began and each has contributed to making the Awards what they are today.

Our final thanks go to the organisations featured in this book – in agreeing to take part, they have allowed us to bring their success stories to a wider audience so that others may learn their secrets.

Moira Clark and Susan Baker

About the authors

Moira Clark is Director of the CRM Research Forum and Senior Lecturer in Marketing at Cranfield School of Management, Cranfield University. She also serves as a consultant to a number of leading international companies. Her major areas of research and consulting are in customer relationship management, relationship marketing and the drivers of customer retention. Moira is a judge for the prestigious Unisys/Management Today Service Excellence Awards. She is also a frequent keynote speaker at many public and in-company seminars and conferences around the world.

Susan Baker is Director of the New Marketing Research Group and Senior Lecturer in Marketing at Cranfield School of Management, Cranfield University. At Cranfield, Susan specialises in consumer marketing and in particular understanding consumer markets, branding and international marketing. A regular contributor to conferences and seminars, at Cranfield she teaches on the MBA programme and works on a variety of management development programmes for companies across all sectors – consumer, business-to-business and professional services. She is a judge in the annual Unisys/Management Today Service Excellence Awards.

Chapter 1

Managing service excellence

Introduction

Service excellence has grown in importance in recent years for a number of significant reasons. First, customers have become increasingly demanding in their service requirements. They experience excellent service at the supermarket and therefore see no reason why they should not get the same from their bank. They know what they want and will often go to great lengths to achieve it. Customers are also much more sophisticated and understand their consumer rights in ways that were not dreamt of in previous generations. Today there is a steady stream of consumer programmes and newspaper and magazine editorial advising them of their rights and how they should go about securing them. This has given rise to more confident consumers, who are not afraid to challenge companies when they receive poor service. Television programmes such as the BBC's Watchdog and consumer magazines like *Which?* have undoubtedly contributed to this better educated consumer society. For companies, this means having to respond to customer demands in ways that impact on their whole business, not just on customer facing personnel.

Secondly, more and more markets are becoming 'commodity' markets. One could argue that one washing machine is much like another and one bank is much like another, as customers perceive few technical differences between competing offerings. Thus, the need to create differential advantage through added value has become vitally important and service excellence is a significant source of that added value. Thirdly, companies are beginning to realise that increases in customer satisfaction and customer retention can have a significant impact on company profitability and corporate success. They are keen to understand what drives service excellence and to know how they can develop a culture and climate that fosters a customer-centric approach to business. Successful companies understand that employee satisfaction and employee behaviour play a pivotal role in determining the level of service quality that is experienced by customers, and hence their level of satisfaction and willingness to remain with the company or to defect.

Despite the fact that service excellence provides companies with such obvious advantages as a capability to meet customer needs, sustainable competitive advantage and improvements in company profitability, it is surprising that service excellence activities generally do not meet customers' expectations or even boardroom aspirations. In many companies the customer has become a nuisance whose unpredictable activities upset standardised business routines. In such companies, customer care practices are usually reactive 'fire fighting' activities. Customer service is often nothing more than complaints handling rather than relationship building, and such organisations are not proactive in developing customer care initiatives that are centred on the customer.

This assumes, of course that customers complain in the first place. Studies show that most dissatisfied customers do not complain to the company when they receive poor service and that 90 per cent will not return in future. So what do customers do instead? They tell each other about their poor service experiences. The power of word of mouth marketing is extraordinary when it comes to service excellence. Basically, on average, customers on the receiving end of poor service will tell ten people about their bad experiences while those who receive great service will, on average, tell only three people. This means that many companies face an uphill struggle in trying to achieve a reputation for service excellence. If companies get the service wrong, everyone will know about it, but if they get it right only three people will hear the news. Of course, with the advent of the Internet, companies have to be even more careful about their service standards to avoid finding themselves the subject of a terrorist web site. Whether you are a car company or a fast food chain, discovering that you have become the focus of your customers' anger and aggression to the extent that they have taken the time and trouble to post their stories on a purpose built terrorist web site, can harness the attention of many a company executive.

What do we mean by service excellence?

For the purposes of this book, service excellence is concerned with an integrated approach to business in which the organisation places the customer at the centre of everything it does. It is about exceeding customer expectations and not just meeting them, and in so doing enabling companies to develop and maintain long-term mutually trusting and profitable relationship with customers. The key words here are 'mutually trusting and profitable'. All customers recognise that companies need to profit from the relationship but they also feel that they themselves should profit as well, in terms of value added services, customer responsiveness and so on. Customers are also increasingly keen to do business with companies that they trust and who they feel will have their interests at heart. A good example of this is the Nationwide Building Society, featured in this book and overall winners of the 2002 Unisys/Management Today Service Excellence Awards. They have now publicly stated that they will offer the same competitive rate mortgages to their existing customers as they do to first time buyers, at a time when most of their competitors only focus on giving the good deals to new customers.

The objective, then, of any organisation is to move customers up the 'staircase of loyalty' (Figure 1.1). In this way, new customers are turned into regularly purchasing clients, who are then progressively moved through the organisation from being strong supporters of the company and its products and services to being active and vocal advocates, where they can play an important role as a source of referrals. The final stage of relationship development is 'partner' where there is a mutually sharing relationship with a supplier. The principal mechanism used for turning prospects into long-term advocates or partners is the provision of service excellence. Of course at any stage on the staircase of loyalty, the relationship with a customer can deteriorate and the customer can become 'dissatisfied', or even a 'terrorist'. A 'dissatisfied' customer may not be happy with the product or service, they may even complain to their supplier, but they are likely to be mostly passive in their response to their dissatisfaction. A 'terrorist', on the other hand, is outspoken and active. They are

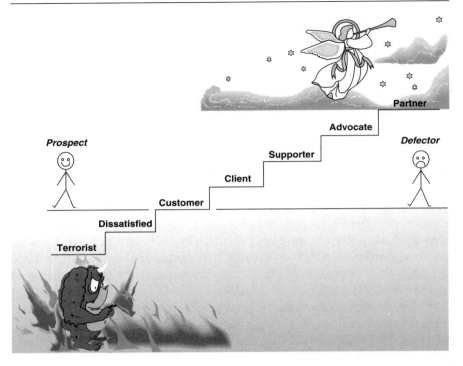

Figure 1.1   The staircase of loyalty

likely to tell as many people as possible about their poor experiences and inflict as much damage as possible on the company in question.

In order to become a service excellent organisation, companies need to be clear about the direction and culture of their business, and how successfully their leadership and values create a passion for customers. For it is only with such clarity of vision that truly high performing companies can thrive and grow. Leadership and values are the bedrock of the Service Excellence Awards as they create a foundation in the business that helps to direct all the activities of the business in an integrated and effective way. Figure 1.2 shows a model of the Service Excellence Awards with 'leadership and values' providing the glue that cements all the other activities that we associate with service excellence and which are the concern of this book, namely: 'customer intelligence', how companies can build an understanding of the needs and expectations of their customers; 'operational effectiveness', how companies deliver promises to customers and 'engaging people', how well a company inspires the hearts and minds of people up and down the organisation to deliver great

Figure 1.2   The service excellence model

service. At the centre of the model is 'organisational agility'. This is concerned with how companies anticipate and respond to the changing environment on an organisation wide basis.

Each of these activities is discussed in detail in this book but it should be remembered that to become a truly service excellent organisation, companies need to adopt a holistic approach to managing these activities. For example, it is no good being superb at customer intelligence if staff are not interested in delivering great service. Likewise, it is no good having great leadership and values if no one understands how to deliver this vision to the customer. This is why being recognised as a service excellence company is so prestigious, because there are no quick fixes, and there are no easy wins. The companies that are discussed in this book have all worked tirelessly and often for some considerable time to achieve their success. Many have entered the awards year on year, measuring their progress as they go. Happy Computers, for example won the 'Business-to-Business' Award in 2002, and then went on to win the overall award in 2003. The Happy Computers case study is featured in Chapter 5.

Why a book on service excellence?

The Service Excellence Awards are organised by Unisys in association with Management Today magazine and are supported by a number of partners including Cranfield School of Management. Cranfield is closely associated with the awards and has supported them for the past seven years, providing judges for the various industry categories as well as ongoing feedback on the awards process and questionnaire design. The authors of this book are two of those judges. In our capacity as judges we have seen behind the scenes at some of the best service excellence companies in the UK today. However, just seeing these companies is not enough; we feel that in our role as business school academics we should try to share our insights and experiences with a wider community so that others may learn the secrets of service excellence success.

The inspiration for this book came during the awards ceremony in 2000 as the TNT Director of Quality, Chris Fowkes, was making his acceptance speech, having won the coveted prize of overall winner. He recounted how the previous year he had heard a speech from an organisation that was keen to make quality improvements but could not afford a budget of more than £100 per employee suggestion of staff to do so. Having heard this, Fowkes thought what an excellent idea it was and proceeded to implement the same strategy of high achieving improvements at low cost. While he was retelling this story, rumblings were to be heard on a nearby table, where people were saying 'that was us, that was us!' Fowkes went on to say that his inspiration for this excellent idea was also in the room. It was, in fact, Foxdenton School and independent nursery for children with special needs (now called the Kingfisher School) who were public sector finalists in 1999, 2000 and 2001. Fowkes then proceeded to thank the staff at the school for teaching such a large company like TNT a thing or two about service quality and went on to detail how much money such an initiative had saved them (see Chapter 3 for the TNT case study).

With this in mind, we decided that if a company like TNT can learn from a small school like Foxdenton, how many more companies could benefit from other service excellence experiences? So our aims in writing this book are to:

- guide organisations to future success by helping them to understand what the key ingredients of service excellence are;
- help organisations develop in ways they can be proud of and that will provide them with sustainable competitive advantage for the future.

About the Unisys/Management Today Service Excellence Awards

The Service Excellence Awards were established with two main object-ives in mind to:

- identify and recognise those organisations operating in the UK that are industry leaders at serving customers;
- help organisations identify their strengths and weaknesses, and provide benchmarks and guidance to help them improve performance.

In the eight years they have been running almost a thousand com-panies that have benefited from the awards process. For the winners and the shortlisted companies these awards enhance their reputa-tions as proven providers of exemplary levels of service excellence. This public recognition also boosts the morale and pride of the staff working in these companies, giving them well-earned credit for being leaders in their field.

The way the process works is that companies enter the awards by completing a self-assessment questionnaire. There is a reproduction of the contents of the 2003 Unisys/Management Today Service Excellence Awards self-assessment questionnaire in Appendix 1. It is also available online at www.serviceexcellenceawards.com. The questionnaire examines each of the five vectors of service excellence through a series of opinion-based statements, data gathering ques-tions and prompts for evidence of best practice. The five vectors are: customer intelligence, operational effectiveness, engaging people, leadership and values and organisational agility. Once the question-naires have been submitted they are subjected to a detailed assess-ment and tailored benchmark reports are prepared for all entrants so that they are able to accurately assess their current performance not only against companies within their sector, but against companies across all sectors. Figures 1.3 and 1.4 show an example of the service excellence vector benchmarks that each entry receives.

These benchmarks help to identify areas needing attention and bring a fresh perspective to service improvement initiatives. From this analysis a shortlist of companies is then identified. These finalists may then be asked to provide further supporting evidence and they each receive a half-day site visit from a team of judges. While visiting each finalist, the judges seek to validate and explore any of the supporting

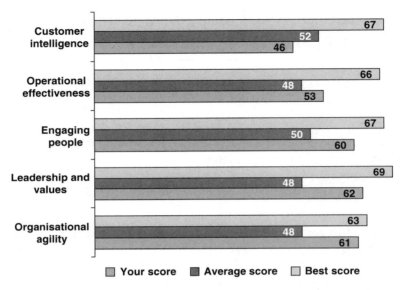

Figure 1.3   Service excellence vector benchmarks – business-to-business entrants

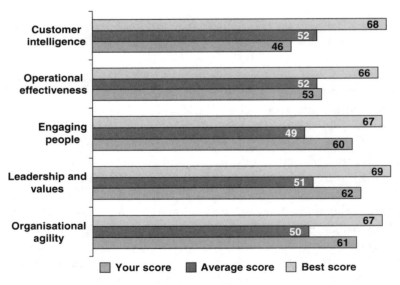

Figure 1.4   Service excellence vector benchmarks – all entrants

evidence presented in their submission. Where possible, these site visits are also supplemented by the judges undertaking some mystery shopping activity. Following these visits, the winners for the award categories and the overall award are then selected from these visits.

The Service Excellence Awards are open to all organisations, large and small. Whether a company is in the public or private sector they can enter in one of the five main award categories:

- Business-to-business services – including logistics and business services.
- Retail and consumer services – includes travel and utilities.
- Financial services – includes banks, building societies, insurance and investment services.
- Manufacturing/engineering – includes construction and process industries.
- Public services – including government, education and not-for-profit organisations.

Awards are made in each category, as well as an award for the best overall organisation. In addition, a Learning Organisation Award is sponsored by Cranfield School of Management, and this is given to the company that has shown the greatest progress towards service excellence, measured by ongoing participation in the awards programme. The awards programme is further endorsed by the 'Fit for the Future' campaign, a CBI-led and government-backed campaign to encourage the transfer of best practice.

The structure of the book

This book contains seven chapters and is structured around the key vectors of service excellence. Chapter 1, this chapter, provides an overview of service excellence and an introduction to the Service Excellence Awards in terms of what they are and how they work. Chapters 2–6, focus in turn on each of the five vectors of service excellence, namely:

- *Customer intelligence*: This chapter examines how a company builds an understanding of the needs and expectations of its customers and how this is used to inform strategy making.
- *Operational effectiveness*: This chapter looks at how organisations deliver their promise to customers. It addresses the effectiveness of service delivery processes and how easy the company is to do business with.
- *Engaging people*: This chapter explores how well a company inspires the hearts and minds of people up and down the organisation to deliver great service.
- *Leadership and values*: This chapter assesses the direction and culture of an organisation, and how successfully the values and leadership create a passion for customers.

- *Organisational agility*: This chapter addresses how well an organisation anticipates and responds to the changing world.

Each chapter is structured around the five key statements that are used in the awards scheme to assess how well companies address each of these issues in their organisations. Table 1.1 shows a list of the 25 'best practice' statements within the self-assessment questionnaire (five per vector) along with the average scores recorded in the 2003 awards by all entrants. These average scores are based on a scale of 1 (low implementation) to 5 (high implementation) for each 'best practice' statement.

Table 1.1 'Best practice' statements

Customer intelligence	
We encourage and act on feedback from customers	4.55
We understand the drivers of customer satisfaction	3.78
We are recognised as innovators in our market	3.99
We build long term, profitable relationships in our chosen markets	3.83
We monitor and track customer retention and repurchase intention	3.56
Operational excellence	
Customers consider us easy to do business with	3.64
We enhance business performance through continuous improvement	4.09
We can deal effectively with customers over multiple channels	4.46
We deal with service failures effectively	4.12
We use the web to enhance the customer's experience	2.94
Engaging people	
People have the right skills and knowledge to do jobs	4.00
We regularly monitor employee satisfaction and act on the findings	3.26
We recognise performance and behaviour of outstanding individuals and teams	3.42
We empower people to deliver service excellence	3.87
When recruiting and developing people we focus on attitudes first	2.27
Leadership and values	
Values are widely understood and practised	3.76
Leadership reflects the organisation's values	3.81
Our processes of management reflect our values	4.36
Senior managers actively champion customers	4.31
We invest in developing leadership across the organisation	3.71
Organisational agility	
Constructive criticism is an essential element of our culture	4.14
The organisation provides methods, tools and training to enable change	3.74
We have tools and techniques that facilitate the capture and sharing of knowledge and expertise	3.44
The organisation monitors and shares information about the changing socio-economic environment	3.44
Our people respond positively to change	4.01

Chapters 2–6 each contains two case studies taken from winners of the Service Excellence Awards over the past 4 years. In choosing the organisations to include in the book we have selected a cross-section from different industry sectors as well as organisations that are particularly good examples of the five vectors of service excellence. Finally, Chapter 7 takes an integrative approach to service excellence and uses the Nationwide Building Society to highlight how this company has achieved success.

A summary of the cases included in the book and the dates, in brackets, that the companies won their awards is shown in Table 1.2. (See page 12.)

Table 1.2 Service Excellence Award winners case studies featured in this book

Chapter No./ title	Business-to-business services	Retail and consumer services	Financial services	Manufacturing/ engineering	Public services	Small business
2 Customer intelligence	Rackspace (2003)	Woburn Safari Park (2002/2003)				
3 Operational effectiveness	TNT Express Services (Business-to-Business winner and overall winner 1997 and 2000)				Dental Practice Board (2002)	
4 Engaging people		PetCareCo (Consumer Services winner 1997 and 2001 and Small Company winner 1997 and 1998)		John Pring & Son (2002)		
5 Leadership and values	Cragrats Limited (Business-to-Business winner and overall winner 2001)					Happy Computers (Overall and small Business winner 2003 and Business-to-Business winner 2002)
6 Organisational agility				BAA plc The Fit Out Team (2001)	The Veterans Agency (2001)	
7 Service excellence best practice			Nationwide Building Society (Financial Services 2000, 2002 and overall winner 2002)			

Chapter 2

Customer intelligence

Introduction

The lifeblood of any organisation is the information it generates about its customers, and the test of organisational longevity is how it then uses this to inform the strategy making process. Organisations today demonstrate a greater willingness than previously to listen to their customers (whoever they may be) and employ a variety of means to achieve this. Many work with traditional research techniques and these may include standard surveys and focus groups. Others, however, go beyond a traditional approach in their search for more innovative ways of learning about their customers' needs and expectations. The understanding generated through these approaches enables the organisation to get underneath their customers' skin in ways that provide ever deeper insights into their unarticulated needs, desires and behaviour.

This level of 'customer intimacy' is, many would argue, a necessity in the highly competitive marketplace in which the majority of organisations find themselves operating. Most managers would agree with the view that customers have become more demanding and sophisticated. Customers often have quite precise expectations of the products and services they are seeking and have become bolder in making their requirements known. Management theorists describe the customers who populate today's markets as knowledgeable and active. And as business journalist Alan Mitchell points out in his book, *Right Side Up*, they are 'aware of the rules of the game'. For the organisation, these increasing levels of marketing literacy mean that it has to work harder to acquire and, moreover, to

retain a customer's business. The process starts with building effective mechanisms to capture customer feedback and then using it to
drive changes to products, services and ways of doing business.

This process forms the first vector of the service excellence model.
It is the initial stepping-stone to achieving customer focus that brings
with it profit and growth. When a customer 'does business' with an
organisation, a process of mutual exchange takes place. The customer
gains the benefits they want for the costs they are prepared to with-
stand (and these are not simply price but may include convenience
factors, such as how much personal information they have to give
up and how far they have to travel to get what they want, etc.). For
its part, the organisation has costs to bear relating to the creation and
delivery of the product or service, and will be seeking to make a
profitable return that may go beyond monetary benefit.

This chapter examines the ways in which organisations build their
knowledge and understanding of their customers' needs and
expectations, and how customers perceive the performance of the
organisation. This information provides an essential foundation on
which the organisation can build its offer to customers and affords
an insight into the changes in products and services that customers
may be looking for. It helps provide insight into customer motivations to buy and can supply knowledge and understanding of the
competitive frame within which the organisation operates. This
information can be leveraged through the process of segmentation,
which works to portion the market and identify the most profitable
sectors (however they may be defined) on which to concentrate the
organisation's resources. This process is essential as it enables the
organisation to be confident about the market in which it operates,
providing the answer to the simple but strategic question, 'What
business are we in?'

This chapter

As with the other four chapters directly focusing on the vectors of
the service excellence model, this chapter is structured around the
five key statements that appear in the self-assessment questionnaire
that forms the backbone of the Service Excellence Awards. These are:

- We encourage and act on feedback from customers.
- We understand the drivers of customer satisfaction.

- We are recognised as innovators in our market.
- We build long-term profitable relationships in our chosen markets.
- We monitor and track customer retention and repurchase intention.

The role played by each statement in developing customer service excellence is explained and then demonstrated through case studies of two previous Awards winners: Woburn Safari Park (retail and consumer services) and Rackspace Managed Hosting (business-to-business).

We encourage and act on feedback from customers

Service Excellence Awards winners strive to take an 'outside-in' approach to strategy development, as opposed to an 'inside-out' one, and this starts with having in place mechanisms to collect customer feedback that deliver real insight into customer needs and expectations. Although insight is derived from the obvious, it is not the same as fact. It is the capacity to penetrate deep into customer motivations and enables the organisation to define the value customers are seeking from *their* perspective.

In essence, these organisations seek to develop a dynamic, listening competency. Many do this by employing traditional market research methods, while others make use of more contemporary procedures. Others go further still by utilising a wide portfolio of market sensing techniques, and this palette of options is considered next.

Traditional and contemporary market research

As the staple method of insight generation, market research aims to answer fundamental questions about what makes customers 'tick' so that managers can refine existing market practice. Organisations usually seek to answer the 'who, what, where, when and how' questions through quantitative research, such as surveys. These routinely involve large numbers of respondents, who may be chosen on a quota basis to create a statistically representative selection of the larger customer population, and can be administered in a variety of ways – through postal questionnaires, online, by telephone or face to face. Regardless of how the data is generated, it is as well to remember that quantitative research essentially deals with averages: it tells managers what the average customer wants. To generate more meaningful insight into customer needs, and to uncover the answers to the 'why' question, managers are increasingly turning to a greater use of qualitative approaches.

Qualitative research today is characterised by the use of focus groups, in-depth interviews and mystery-shopper type exercises. These methods involve asking comparatively small samples of respondents questions about what they do and think, and listening to and interpreting the response. The output of this type of research is exploratory, or diagnostic, in nature; respondents are not meant to be representative of the larger population, but are intended to reflect the profile of known or desired customers.

Both of these approaches to market research are based on an assumption that customers can – and are willing to – articulate their thoughts, feelings, beliefs and behaviours. Organisations wanting to make breakthrough developments are rather more concerned with understanding latent, unarticulated customer wants and desires. To meet this demand, researchers have added observation-based methods to their toolbox. These include detailed assessments of customers' behaviour through ethnographic techniques that essentially watch and record customers in their own environment. The Woburn Safari Park case study at the end of this chapter illustrates an innovative way of achieving this that deeply impressed the judges in the 2003 Awards.

Market sensing

Service Excellence Awards winners tend to adopt a wider approach to market sensing however. They take advantage of the benefits of customer relationship management (CRM) installations that are able to generate highly detailed analyses of customer behaviour through the capture of customer data at various points of interaction. This reliance on IT systems is then augmented in some organisations through insight gleaned through frontline staff that is then fed back into the system. Making this work consistently requires open channels of communication within the organisation.

A very effective way of monitoring customer satisfaction is to encourage and collect complaints and compliments. Best practice organisations systematically record, review and use these pieces of information to drive changes in products, services and ways of doing business.

While each of the research approaches outlined here offers part of the solution to better customer intelligence, no one technique delivers the absolute answer. Managers today increasingly adopt what is known as a bricolage approach to customer understanding. This pieces together investigative and interpretive methods drawn from different disciplines, that is, a mix-and-match approach. Customer understanding is not, however, a matter of simply linking together different research techniques but is rather more an organisational attitude of mind. Those who are able to prove that 'this is the way we conduct business' or 'listening to customers is a part of our culture' are best placed for success, as their advantage comes from having a dynamic approach to collecting and acting on customer and market data that is a part of their culture and systems.

We understand the drivers of customer satisfaction

An 'outside-in' approach to strategy development means eschewing a reliance on management intuition to 'know' customers and 'understand' what they are seeking, and developing instead a curiosity about seeing matters from the customer's perspective. In some cases, that can mean seeing things from the customer's *customer's* perspective. In each of these cases, the organisation is attempting to understand the exact nature of the value the customer (or end-user) is seeking.

This concept of value is crucial to customer intelligence and is best envisaged as a set of concentric circles (see Figure 2.1). In the centre

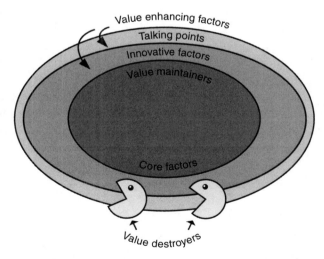

Figure 2.1 The value concept. *Source*: New Consumer Marketing, Susan Baker, 2003 (Wiley)

are the factors that maintain value for customers. These are the 'hygiene' factors, or the core features and attributes that all competitors must offer to be considered players in a particular marketplace. Surrounding these are the 'value enhancers'. These are the key discriminating factors that set the organisation apart from competitors in the eyes of customers. Occasionally, these factors may be 'adopted' by customers and become talking points, creating great word-of-mouth marketing. Organisations offering value enhancers will build market share quickly, rearranging the competitive forces in the marketplace as they do so.

The third set of factors to be identified through customer intelligence systems are those that diminish and destroy value in the customer's eyes. Put simply, these are the 'turn offs' for customers. Once identified, these order losers should be eliminated from the offering.

Having identified the various components of value that factor in the customer's perception of value, the organisation then needs to understand their exact meaning for customers. These may be described by customers in terms of the features and attributes of a product or service, but managers need to understand precisely the nature of the benefits that these features and attributes deliver. In some cases, they may offer higher level, intangible benefits that satisfy certain personal values or business goals (see Figure 2.2). This is where customer satisfaction surveys need to be focused if they are to pick up meaningful data.

Customer intelligence, then, enables the organisation to define value from the customer's perspective. It provides a means of identifying underlying sources of customer motivation. This needs to be set within the wider socio-economic environment so that organisations are alert to trends that may impact on customer motivation. It is also important that organisations appreciate that perceptions of value shift over time and what were once value enhancers with a certain group of customers can quickly become the hygiene factors. Organisations that fail to appreciate this can find their customer satisfaction ratings take a nosedive.

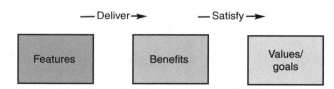

Figure 2.2   The means-end model

We are recognised as innovators in our market

The way to drive up customer satisfaction ratings is to continually innovate not only what the organisation does, but also the way in which it does it. Innovation in service excellence is about creating new solutions that are acknowledged by customers as offering real value. Organisations that achieve this can point to a link between innovation and customer satisfaction and sales.

The word innovation comes from the Latin *innovare*, meaning to renew or alter, and it provides an organisation with a way of creating new value-producing resources or endowing existing ones with an enhanced potential for yielding profit. It is the result of a complex set of processes, involving organisational learning, culture, leadership and management style. This contrasts with popular accounts of innovation that focus on the 'heroic inventor' and their inventions. Much of the academic writing on the innovation process similarly separates invention from innovation, or creativity from its commercial application. The traditional model of innovation is represented as a sequential one, where the process passes through phases of idea generation, invention, research and development and application through to diffusion. It has, however, long been recognised that this linear model is over-simplified and that innovations emerge as a result of a complex, iterative process.

The high failure rate of new product and service launches is well documented and where success does occur, many sectors are characterised by incremental rather than discontinuous, or radical, breakthroughs. Research from Insead Professors Kim and Mauborgne suggests that products and services offering only incremental improvements are likely to generate lower sales and substantially less profitability than truly pioneering innovations. They use the term 'value pioneers' to describe organisations who succeed in managing processes that make competition irrelevant and who create new markets by focusing on what value needs to be produced. For example, Virgin Group is an organisation that has demonstrated time and again how to bring radically new products and services into the marketplace without being the first to market in a particular sector. The company's understanding of the value-adding factors that matter to consumers has enabled it to successfully operate in markets where it has taken on established giants in a 'David versus Goliath' battle for consumer loyalty. For this reason, Virgin has gained a reputation as a challenger brand.

Many organisations mistakenly believe that adding more technology to a product or service will result in value-adding innovation. However, what customers want from technology is new or enhanced value that will extend their abilities and provide them with greater ease of use and convenience. Successful new-to-the-world innovation succeeds because it represents a genuine breakthrough in delivering a value proposition that is based on a deep understanding of the nature of the value customers seek. It is intricately bound to the process of customer intelligence.

We build long-term profitable relationships in our chosen markets

In best practice organisations, customer intelligence is turned into marketing action through the process of segmentation. By segmenting customers into groups sharing the same or similar needs on the basis of value (*their* definition), an organisation can assess where it ought to most profitably focus its resources. And where these customer groups can be tracked over time, this information can be used to refine strategies for relationship management. This approach typifies organisations that take a mindful approach to their market and contrasts with organisations that accept any customer is a good customer.

Much of the current discussion about segmentation is informed by a somewhat mechanistic approach and is characterised by the use of scientific and rational language, which focuses on the way in which the organisation should segment its market, that is, chop it up into manageable chunks. The reality of today's consumption-led economy is that customers themselves unwittingly form loose groups whose members seek the same or similar sets of value factors. In other words, customers segment *their* market and form subgroups with *their* own sets of requirements. As a consequence, the language now associated with segmentation is more to do with creativity and insight, as organisations wrestle with the challenge of finding a means of exposing these segments of customers and defining the value each is seeking.

By leveraging customer intelligence through the process of segmentation, an organisation can be confident about the market in which it operates. It provides an answer to the simple but strategic question 'What business are we in?' Today, too many organisations still define segments in terms of the products and services they offer. Personal financial services companies with a poor reputation for customer service, for example, typically take this product-driven approach, defining segments as 'endowment policies', 'savings bonds' or 'savings accounts'. They fail to understand the kinds of value customers need and expect, such as the desire to save for retirement, to support a child through university or simply to have peace of mind.

Customer databases built up through loyalty card schemes, such as those provided by the major supermarkets, can provide a rich source of information on customer motivation. However, it should always be remembered that a segmentation analysis built solely on this sort of data can only reflect the motivations of existing customers. It becomes a *database* segmentation and not any form of *market* segmentation. Meaningful segmentation analysis takes into consideration different types of data. However, the effective use of CRM systems can enable an organisation to take a dynamic approach to segmentation. Tesco, with its successful Clubcard scheme has a database of over 10 million UK households and is said to be able to distinguish thousands of serviceable segments. This analysis is used to drive the business, so much so that David Reid, Tesco's deputy chairman, has claimed that 'If you took our loyalty cards away from us, it would be like flying blind.'

We monitor and track customer retention and repurchase intention

Best practice service excellence is underscored by a compelling business philosophy that promotes the establishment of long term, mutually trusting and profitable relationships with customers. Known as 'relationship marketing', it evolved as a response to the constrained economic environment of the 1970s and a series of oil crises. The consequent economic downturn, followed by high inflation at home, had a serious impact on customers. Buyer motivations reflected a combination of prudence and sophistication not seen before.

Supplying organisations responded by re-examining what they were offering to customers. To increase product appeal, differentiation and value for money, many augmented their product offerings by incorporating a service element. This spawned the development of services marketing as a business function. In mature markets where the rate of growth had slowed or even stopped, it became more difficult for organisations to pursue a strategy of gaining market share. With the pool of new prospects diminished, marketing attention focused instead on retaining and growing existing customer relationships. Consequently, 'customer loyalty' became a priority, and its strategic importance remains to this day.

The shift in marketing emphasis from customer acquisition to customer retention became enshrined in the principles of relationship marketing. Unlike transaction marketing, relationship marketing recognises that transactions are not isolated events but that they take place within a live and continuous context of engagement – in other words, a 'relationship' between buyer and seller.

Measures of marketing success then turned from numbers of customers (market share) to share of customer expenditure (share of 'wallet') and potential customer value (customer lifetime value). The work of Bain consultants Frederick Reichheld and Earl Sasser was seminal in demonstrating the large impact on profitability of small increases in customer retention rates. Further research showed the increasing profitability of customers the longer the relationship lasts, and added strength to the argument for a relationship marketing approach. Towards the end of the 1990s the development of IT-driven CRM systems offered the promise of implementing relationship marketing effectively. The theory behind CRM is that managing customer relationships is an integrated business process involving the consolidation of individual customer data from multiple sources to create a mutually valuable proposition.

The potency of relationship marketing and CRM is demonstrated by the fact that they have been adopted across both the commercial and not-for-profit sectors. This is because the core of a relationship marketing approach is that customers are recognised and their previous history is remembered. For commercial organisations, working at a high level of sophistication, this enables them to predict retention and repurchase intention, and assess the financial impact of these. While not-for-profit organisations, many of whom operate in the public sector where reuse of services is not wanted or needed, nonetheless find they are able to work successfully with the principles behind the philosophy. The Dental Practice Board and The Veterans Agency are offered as cases in point here, in Chapters 3 and 6 respectively.

Summary points

- An outside-in approach to strategy development enables the organisation to define the value customers are seeking from the *customer's* perspective.

- No one research tool or technique provides absolute customer intelligence – organisations need to blend a portfolio of methods in an ongoing process.
- Organisations need to understand how customer value is made up: the elements that maintain value, the value enhancers and the value destroyers.
- Innovation in service excellence is about creating new solutions (in *how* the organisation does something as much as *what* it does) that are acknowledged by customers as offering real value.
- Customer intelligence is made actionable through the process of segmentation, which helps the organisation answer the question 'what business are we in?'
- Service excellence is underscored by a compelling business philosophy that promotes the establishment of long term, mutually trusting and profitable relationships with customers.

Further reading

Wendy Gordon (1999). *Goodthinking – A Guide to Qualitative Research*. Admap.
David Smith and Jonathan Fletcher (2001). *Inside Information*. Wiley.
Malcolm McDonald and Ian Dunbar (1998). *Market Segmentation: How To Do It; How To Profit From It*. Macmillan.

Best practice cases

Introduction

The illustrative cases in this chapter have been selected for demonstrating best practice in generating customer intelligence and the way in which this is used to drive customer service strategies. Woburn Safari Park (overall winners of the retail and consumer services sector in 2000, highly commended in 2002 and overall winners again in 2003), is a part of the Woburn estate in Bedfordshire. The case relates how Chief Executive Chris Webster has led a turn around in the prevailing culture, which has seen the staff's passion for the animals extended to customers. Woburn Safari Park is now as much a centre for conservation and education as a popular tourist resort. The business has grown dramatically over the past decade and has at the heart of its strategy making a commitment to generating meaningful customer intelligence. As the management actions during the crippling foot-and-mouth crisis reveal, there is also an entrepreneurial spirit at large which enables the organisation to turn adversity to advantage.

The second case study focuses on Rackspace Managed Hosting which manages the servers that keep hundreds of web sites running smoothly for customers who sit in the UK, Europe and as far away as India. While Rackspace's staff rarely meet their end-users, they nonetheless have a passionate commitment to providing the highest possible standards of customer service. So much so, that the organisation has trademarked the name it gives to this process – Fanatical Support. Not surprisingly the outcome is outstanding levels of customer satisfaction, low churn rates and spectacular business growth. Driving this is a desire on the part of 'Rackers', the name staff give to themselves, to understand their customers' every need and the company employs a number of techniques for ensuring this insight is captured and communicated around the business. In 2003 Rackspace was awarded the Learning Organisation Award.

Woburn Safari Park

Introduction

Woburn Safari Park has won a Service Excellence Award three times in four years, demonstrating an extraordinary consistency in impressing several sets of judges. Originally opened in 1970 as a franchise by the Chipperfield family, this popular visitor attraction has journeyed along a curve of initial novelty, through an extended period of commercial doldrums, and into a new era of renewed success as a leading exemplar of environmental conservation.

The Park's mission is no longer about showing the public a collection of exotic animals: the proposition for the twenty-first century combines a great day out with awareness of environmental issues. Woburn Safari Park has come a long way from its original circus industry founders – and is establishing new standards of customer insight and service.

The need for a turnaround

The concept of a safari park in the depths of the gentle English countryside was novel and entrepreneurial in its time. But greater access to foreign travel, alongside advances in the way the natural world is presented to audiences on television, have made what was exotic everyday. At the same time growing awareness of ecological issues, and mankind's relationship with the plants and animals with which we share the planet, has changed public perceptions of nature as a spectacle to be tamed and contained for our amusement. In terms of hard metrics, visitor numbers declined as the attraction aged. The Chipperfield franchise came to an end in 1993, and Woburn Abbey's custodians appointed Chris Webster as the Park's new leader.

With his background in the military and in marketing, Webster quickly saw a connection between low staff morale and customer dissatisfaction. Staff attitudes seemed to be inward-facing, with little sense of team objectives. Each keeper was responsible for looking after his animals and felt no need to acknowledge or understand his colleagues' roles. A 'blame culture' was evident, as was the feeling that visitors were simply a nuisance who disturbed the animals. While the staff's overriding concern for the animals was valuable and well intentioned, it was not aligned with the Park's commercial interests. The decline in visitor numbers also threatened the very existence of the attraction, and therefore the animals' long-term well-being. The poor state of staff morale also led to problems in keeping the team up to strength.

Webster began the Park's climb back to effectiveness by communicating the vital bond between visitors and animals. He showed Woburn's people that without a serious focus on customer care, the future of the animals at the Park was being put at risk.

Webster's analysis of the Park's state showed that the product offering – the Safari Park experience itself – was not meeting customer needs. Customer expectations had risen since 1970, with customers now more sophisticated and demanding. They were also more ready to compare the value for money they received at Woburn with alternative family activities.

Putting the 'WOW factor' back into the business

Woburn Safari Park was seen as tired and overpriced when compared to competing forms of entertainment. The average length of customer stay was only 2.5 hours. Webster's research also made it plain that each customer was looking for a good day out. The product desperately needed to connect with customers and deliver that elusive 'WOW factor'.

The Park's turnaround began with a renewal of the staffing strategy. Staffing levels were ramped up and recruitment shifted to values-based selection criteria. Selection focused on people who were confident in customer-facing roles while sharing a passion for animal welfare and conservation.

A programme of cultural change was launched in order to break down barriers among existing staff and show them the importance of customer care. Gradually a 'can-do' culture took over at Woburn, with each employee encouraged to interact with the customer and become a kind of walking information post. Team members also developed their cultural awareness and sensitivity to help them interact more effectively with visitors from all backgrounds.

Reorienting the team towards respect for people as well as animals was the first step in rebuilding the attraction. But connecting with customers takes more than mere recognition of their existence. The Park's management also had to find out what its customers wanted of the attraction, and how the Park's existing and potential capabilities could be marshalled to deliver the 'good day out' people wanted of Woburn.

The importance of segmentation

A series of focus groups was run to discover customers' wants and needs. The focus group programme was supplemented with annual visitor surveys. Internal staff surveys were established to ensure the team's insights and ideas were added to the data. The Park also used mystery shoppers to glean detailed customer experiences in a controlled format.

Chris Webster next appointed a Marketing Manager to lead the task of better understanding customer motivations and targeting the market more accurately. A segmentation scheme was soon in place, allowing the business to decide on its priority targets for the Park's regeneration. Tight resources meant management had to focus on those segments that would provide a speedy and high return. A key target was children under 12 and their families – including grand-parents. Local community groups and schools were also identified as prime target segments.

As the Park's experience with segmentation has grown, the team has become more sophisticated in using it. Micro-segmentation has created special price offers for mothers with children visiting after school hours, as well as half-price tickets for local people. Such ini-tiatives serve the dual purposes of attracting visitors and genera-ting positive word-of-mouth recommendations. Micro-segmentation analysis also identified opportunities to attract non-traditional visi-tors who might otherwise not experience the Park. Older visitors with time on their hands and travel concessions are one key group, while parents with children who have left home represent another group. The Park can develop relationships with these groups in visits outside of the school term-time peak season, when staff have more time to interact with them and the Park's atmosphere is calmer. Above all, using segmentation helped the team appreciate the diversity of modern family structures and leisure pursuits. These insights enable the team to develop family activities with genuine appeal to prospective visitors. Woburn's offer is now firmly built around concepts of customer drivers, rather than a simple show-and-tell.

Innovation in strategy development

Woburn continues to exploit new channels of communication with its customers. It has run an interactive web site since 2001, allowing the Park to continue its education goals beyond the physical visit as well as engage in extended dialogues with customers. The web site attracts an average of 859 visitors per day, each of whom spends an average of 6.16 minutes at the site. The web site acts as an effective sales channel, allowing customers to buy tickets online. Currently 13 per cent of visitors leave an e-mail address with the Park as their preferred method of communication.

Changes to the Park's approach to customers are also reflected in its product portfolio. The Safari Club scheme allows members to visit the Park whenever they like during the year. Members also receive a Safari newsletter informing them of the latest upcoming events at the Park. The Park's Safari Lodge has been opened up to customer bookings for parties and corporate events, making Woburn Safari Park a multi-purpose destination. But the animals have not been forgotten amidst the changes. Members of the public can now adopt an animal, helping to pay for its care and welfare. The Park also runs special days centred around animal care and behaviour themes, such as elephant washing and keeper shadowing.

One of Woburn's most innovative ideas for involving customers is the Junior Board. As the development of environmental awareness is central to the Park's vision, and the environmental awareness of children currently outstrips that of the older generation, it makes sense to give children a voice in the running and future of the park. Children are also of course key customers, and significant influencers on families' leisure activity decisions.

Members of the Junior Board are recruited from the children in the Safari Club and annual ticket holders. An Educational Officer, who is also a qualified teacher, interviews potential board members, most of whom are around age 11. The Junior Board meets twice a term and is used as a focus group for idea generation. Board members visit other attractions and leisure destinations to benchmark the experiences against Woburn's offering. The Junior Board also chooses an environmental project to support and raise funds for each year. The young Board members are naturally curious, direct and vocal – and a great source of inspiration beyond the reach of traditional market research techniques.

The results of the new customer-focused strategy speak for themselves. Visitor numbers nearly doubled from 173,000 in 1992 to 330,000 in 2000. Turnover quadrupled over the same period. These remarkable achievements were key to the Park's Service Excellence Award for 2000.

The challenge of competitive threats

But the market – and nature – are no respecters of awards. 2001 saw major challenges in the form of convincing competition and the national epidemic of foot-and-mouth disease. As Chris Webster says: 'Other wildlife attractions are not our only form of competition. We are competing against all forms of leisure activities. Even the shopping centre in Milton Keynes has become a form of leisure activity.'

Nearby Milton Keynes is also home to Gulliver's Kingdom, which attracted visitors away from the Park when it opened for business. A popular television docusoap made at Whipsnade Zoo similarly enticed a number of visitors away from Woburn. The millennium celebrations and the considerable media attention given to London's Millennium Dome also depressed Woburn's visitor numbers. Meanwhile government restrictions intended to contain foot-and-mouth disease led to the closure of the Park for 13 weeks. The Park opened a retail outlet in Milton Keynes to keep the attraction's name in the public's consciousness.

The Park's reopening gave the team the opportunity to collect visitors' home postcodes, partly to satisfy foot-and-mouth regulations and partly to improve Woburn's geodemographic model of the customer base. The Park continues to grow its understanding of customers through data collection. Of the total 740,000 customers who visited during 2002/2003, Woburn has records for 30,000. This collection shows it is possible to convert casual visitors into members of a community. All visitors are invited to complete a survey at the exit gate, rating what they have experienced during their visit.

Chris Webster sees plenty of room for growth in Woburn's business, and recalls the downturn of 2000/2001 as a temporary setback. 2002 was the Park's best year ever, with a total of 417,000 visitors and turnover of £5.3 million. Return on Investment for 2002 was calculated at 31 per cent, and staff received a profit-related bonus of 10 per cent at Christmas. Membership of the Safari Club increases by 30 per cent per year, while group bookings have seen a 25 per cent increase. The Park has been able to increase its peak entry price by £1 without customer resistance.

The role of vision

Webster believes the key to the Park's long-term success lies in the words of its vision: 'The challenge is to become the leader in the conservation sector.' He notes that the British public is becoming more environmentally aware, but is not yet on a par with other European nations. Wildlife attractions in the Netherlands, for example, attract on average around 700,000 visitors per year, from a smaller population than that of the UK. Webster conducted a study tour in the US and discovered that Americans tend to be more in touch with nature than Britons. He believes Woburn needs to engage with the public at a deeper level in order to emulate the more significant role that outdoor attractions play in the Netherlands or in the US. Part of this mission is to promote the view that outdoor activities help children learn vital skills for adulthood, through the emotional and physical challenges of interaction in a natural setting.

Meanwhile day-to-day life at the Park continues to offer authentic, customer-focused experiences. It is the millions of small 'wow moments' that combine to create a robust, living brand. All staff are empowered to respond to customer disappointments by offering them alternative experiences, ensuring visitors not only remain satisfied customers, but become enthusiastic advocates of the Park. Written complaints halved after the cultural changes took hold. A recent survey found that 64 per cent of active customers would visit the Park again, and 76 per cent would recommend Woburn as a destination to others.

Generating deeper insights

Woburn's team have confirmed the grass roots success of their customer strategies, and gathered further fuel for change, through a 2002 research study dubbed Vision Experience. This project included personal sessions with 200 individual customers and 200 family groups. It also included a 'tagging' exercise, in which 20 families were continuously monitored during their visit to the Park. The information gleaned by Vision Experience was detailed and precise, revealing clear areas for improvement. For example, the study showed that customers tended to spend 45 minutes in the Park's restaurant, but an hour on picnics. This is vital data for the remodelling of the Park's catering approach. The study also produced a model of traffic flow through the Park, identifying bottlenecks and leading to a rethink of the miniature railway. Bottleneck areas are now targeted by additional live demonstrations from keepers, so that waiting time is converted into valued customer experience.

The close connection between attending to customer needs and changing the Park's offering is a virtuous circle, and a process rooted in practicality. This approach chimes with another strand of Webster's vision: that of offering an alternative to the 'hyperreality' of modern theme parks. While high-tech theme parks can impress with manufactured experiences, the spread of technology in our lives makes real nature all the more precious. Webster feels that as the number of animals living in the wild continues to decline, places like Woburn Safari Park will become vital resources. With human society continuing to squeeze the space available to untamed nature, a well-managed and conservation-sensitive location such as Woburn becomes an important haven. Combining this ecological mission with the goal of providing a truly special family day will generate strong and enduring consumer appeal.

Work is underway to connect this vision with a stronger Woburn brand. 'Woburn Safari Park is more than just a business,' says Chris Webster. 'It has a responsibility to put something back into society.'

Rackspace Managed Hosting

Introduction

As the technical barriers to market entry in high-tech industries fall, the commercial bar continues to rise. The hosting market is one such business area where the apparent price of joining the fray shrivels in the face of the efforts needed to stand out from competitors. Hosting computer systems for business customers might look at first sight like a commodity business, but it is really all about customer service. Sheds full of servers, humming quietly and turning an efficient revenue turbine while the owners sleep? Think instead of the people who rely on those servers for the health of *their* businesses: people who have entrusted a key part – and often the only part – of their business infrastructure to a team who claims they can do it better than anyone else. Rackspace is a hosting solutions company that majors in people as well as machines, winning plaudits from industry admirers and delighted customers alike.

The importance of the human touch

Rackspace's customer intelligence strategy begins at the company's web site. While many commercial web sites offer interactive features, these are often limited to form-filling. Rackspace has a proactive chat facility that connects visitors directly to a Rackspace team member. Any visitor to the site is likely to see a window pop up with a friendly welcome typed in real time by a named individual. The visitor can then engage directly in conversation with the team member. This means that Rackspace customers and prospects can interact with the company in an unstructured way, using informal language and without having to navigate the company's site. It is also a very powerful way of giving the company a human presence. The chat window immediately reassures the visitor that Rackspace is staffed by real, live human beings who are there to meet customer needs. The web site attracts around 8000 visitors per month, and the company aims to chat with most of them. Rackspace tries to turn 25 per cent of those conversations into sales leads.

If customers need further reassurance that Rackspace has a material presence as well as a virtual one, they are welcome to visit the company's data centres. Customers can see the facility and chat to the people on the team. This creates a long-term image of the company in the customer's mind, which can then be reactivated during subsequent interactions over the phone. The company holds a sales event once every two months, to which the team invites its top customers plus a selection from the rest of the customer base. Events have included yachting at Cowes, meals in top London restaurants, and the send-off of Concorde in October 2003. 'People drive hundreds of miles just to have a drink with us,' says Dominic Monkhouse, Managing Director of Rackspace.

Fanatical Support

The key to Rackspace's differentiation is what the company calls Fanatical Support. Rackspace people are highly motivated towards satisfying customer needs, and exceeding them wherever possible. Customer David Wilkinson of Avenida Technologies is a fan of Rackspace's fanaticism. 'They're fabulous – my first recommendation in hosting solutions,' says Wilkinson. 'I don't enthuse easily, but when I do …

For example, my server crashed a couple of months ago. They spotted it, diagnosed a motherboard failure and had it fixed and up and running within around 40 minutes. I never even noticed until they emailed me to tell me.

This kind of proactivity ensures that Rackspace's service has a legendary quality that is constantly renewed by positive customer experiences. It also enables the company to maintain a learning posture towards its customers, since it is not reliant on customer complaints as a driver of the relationship. And the genuine warmth felt by its customers for the company infects every aspect of the enterprise's activities, right the way through to sales. 'You know that what you are selling is genuinely the best out there,' says Sales Executive Jen Bagshaw. 'When we say 95 per cent of our customers are delighted with our service, we know it's true. We all see the evidence.'

So what is Fanatical Support? 'A customer service program so unique, we trademarked it!' according to the company's web site. In practical terms, Rackspace is upfront in its belief that reliable servers, secure data centres and plentiful bandwidth are not the key to hosting enterprise-class web sites and applications. Rackspace regards hosting primarily as a service, not just a collection of technologies. The Fanatical Support philosophy reflects the company's goal to bring responsiveness and value to everything it does for its customers. The Fanatical Support experience kicks in at the moment a Rackspace team member answers the phone and begins to interact with the company, and extends through every point of interaction.

But Fanatical Support is not a basket of warm feelings. It also contains some very tough guarantees. For example, Rackspace guarantees 100 per cent network uptime. In case that isn't clear, they confirm that 'this amounts to 0 seconds of downtime per month'. Rackspace undertakes to identify and fix hardware failures within 1 hour, as customer David Wilkinson found out. And it goes without saying that Fanatical Support is available from live team members 24 hours per day, seven days per week.

Each customer is assigned a dedicated Fanatical Support team to manage the daily operations of its hosting environment. Each team works with only a handful of customers so that team members become familiar with each customer's specific system set-up and can quickly identify and resolve issues. The company has 350 employees across the group, the majority of whom are directly involved in providing Fanatical Support. As the business continues to grow and gain experience its skills and knowledge base also grow, meaning that Rackspace's value to its customers continually increases.

Segmentation strategy

The support team structure reflects Rackspace's segmentation strategy, which Monkhouse says is 'constantly a work in progress'. Continuous exploration of customer needs and preferences drives the segmentation. The current model has four groups. The first is for virtual hosting customers. These customers resell domains or run applications or e-commerce sites on behalf of other parties. The second group is for 'dedicated business'. These customers use Rackspace as a turnkey IT facility, running their facilities from Rackspace-supplied control panels. Most customers in this group tend to be hobbyists or startup enterprises – a distinction which tends to blur creatively in the Internet business. Dedicated business customers are highly price-sensitive.

The third segment represents Rackspace's core business. These customers buy managed hosting from Rackspace. They have their own servers, and Fanatical Support as standard. They are assured human contact whenever they need it. Rackspace does not use automated phone response systems. 'There's none of that "press 2 to commit suicide" stuff,' says Monkhouse, poking fun at the obstructive systems some customer services organisations have put in place.

Rackspace's fourth customer segment is enterprise customers. There is clearly an overlap between managed hosting customers and enterprise customers. But customers are considered to belong to the enterprise group according to their own purchase decisions. Buying added value services promotes managed hosting customers into this category. The key to this group's definition is therefore not the size or reputation of the customer's organisation, but the demonstrated value they put on their IT infrastructure.

Maximising customer satisfaction

Rackspace regularly undertakes in-depth research on its customer base. A study carried out in 2003 focused on the demographics of 1000 EMEA customers, and built a valuable picture of the typical customer – yielding results that would never follow from intuition. For example, the study showed that 85 per cent of the UK client base was not the end-user of the systems hosted at Rackspace. In other words, these customers held the relationship with Rackspace but were not the ultimate beneficiaries of the facilities. Such customers tend to be IT services businesses in their own right, selling into specific vertical markets. They tend to have around 50 people, be run by people around 35 years old, and have a value proposition centred on Internet technology. The nature of these businesses means that losing their online presence at any time can damage their reputations and their revenue streams.

Rackspace's research, backed up by its day-to-day conversations with customers, shows that its customer base is technically savvy, and often nursing bad experiences from hosting companies. Forty-five per cent of customers have used a competitor so, as Monkhouse puts it, 'they know the grass isn't greener elsewhere'. A staggering 50 per cent of customers arrive as a result of word-of-mouth recommendation. Many customers start their relationship with Rackspace with a sense of relief, having sat out the tail end of a contract with an unsatisfactory competitor, and already interacted with Rackspace people before they could take up the service.

It is at these crucial changeover points that Rackspace sees the pain its competitors cause to customers, and the compelling value of its own customer service principles. One example is a competitor's inability to offer changes to firewall policy outside normal office hours: Rackspace customers can implement their changes at any time they wish. Rackspace and its customers know that 'normal office hours' is a redundant concept in a connected, globalised business environment. The hosting industry's use of contract periods tends to bottle up customer dissatisfaction and poison relationships in organisations who do not put customer service first on their list of priorities.

Rackspace is proud of its customer satisfaction rates, noting that 99 per cent of customers are either 'satisfied' or 'very satisfied'. But Monkhouse does not see the numbers as any reason for complacency, and detects several areas for action. 'I'm happy with people who give us a five,' he says, 'and I want to turn fours into fives. Ninty-seven per cent of customers say they'd refer us. But when it comes to action on a referral, you need a five-person. Repurchase intention and referral rate can go higher if we target those fours.'

One aspect of increasing customer satisfaction at this micro-level lies in subtly reminding customers of the Rackspace benefits they enjoy, but may not have noticed. For example, customers report that they want named account managers – even though they already have named account managers. As a consequence, the company has altered its hold message to include a reminder that all Rackspace customers have a named contact. Enterprise customers also have a named technical contact, who calls the customer once a week with a proactive review of the account, containing advice and suggestions for changes or upgrades.

Another route to increasing customer satisfaction is to act on customer needs, even where a perfect solution cannot be put in place. For example, a number of the surveyed customers agreed that it would be helpful to know who in Rackspace speaks their mother tongue. The company is now offering its people's language skills to customers, so that a speaker of, say, German will see a link to a German speaker when she goes to Rackspace's web site. There is no pressure for the customer to activate the link, nor does Rackspace make any promise to cover every language group used in the countries of its EMEA area – which extends from the UK to India. But the facility is another sign of the company's helpfulness, and a further expression of its human composition.

Rackspace has embarked on a programme of asking its customers to make referrals, rather than hoping referrals will come around. A symbolic gift campaign – a specially presented jar of coffee – is followed by a phone call.

Customer retention strategies

At the other end of the customer life cycle, Rackspace pays careful attention to retention. Although the company offers a range of contract periods, the typical customer is on a 12-month agreement. When the contract reaches the 9–12 month period, the revenue is at risk. This is the contract's 'horizon'. The customer will have typically used a high degree of support in the early part of the contract, while his systems were bedding in, being tested and modified. This high-touch period is likely to decline at around 3–5 months. This means Rackspace has to target customers for signing a new contract in the 6–9 month window. Monkhouse believes that if you can get customers to buy something in this crucial period, they are unlikely to 'churn' – leave for a competitor.

The team therefore calculates what it calls 'value buckets' for each customer. These allow the account managers to see what Rackspace is prepared to give a customer in order to keep him on board. The value buckets are based on the customer's profitability, which is in turn calculated from their revenue versus the amount of support they have used. This strategy allows account managers to 'save' customers through offers valued by the customers. As Account Manager Sam

Stiborski says: 'People are often just looking for an acknowledgement of their loyalty'.

Rackspace's awareness of the critical repurchase window, and the flexibility it gives itself to delight customers at this crucial time, let it turn potential customer losses into 'wow' experiences. For example, one customer who experienced downtime of 8.5 hours had misunderstood the nature of their contract, believing the company was managing a backup strategy for them. Rackspace put in around £1800 of free support to fix the problem, and added a month's free hosting. It then recommended the customer move to having a second server to mirror their core server, so they would be able to continue running their applications if a fault occurred again. Rackspace's value bucket for this company showed they could give this server to the customer for free – an additional, and welcome, surprise. 'Our evangelists are the people who have had a major failure with our team going through hell to fix it for them,' says Monkhouse.

Customer intelligence is an important ingredient in Rackspace's rapid success. The UK business grew from four people to 30 in two years, hitting a turnover of £5 million from a modest start. The speed of growth is connected to Rackspace's low churn rate: at 1 per cent, it is far ahead of the best competitor's score of 2.5 per cent. Low churn is achieved through intimate engagement with customers, and a determination to do whatever it takes to delight them.

Going the last mile

Reflecting on the success Rackspace is enjoying by using committed customer service principles, it is hard to understand how their competitors survive. Dominic Monkhouse believes most of the company's competitors are stuck with the misapprehension that they are IT businesses rather than service businesses. He also believes that great customer service organisations begin with passionate people. Writing in *Computing* magazine about the difficulties of recruiting, Monkhouse said: 'I hate to say it, but too many techies fit the nerd role. They spend too much time in a darkened room with only a computer for company. And they cannot offer the level of reassurance or comfort that is expected when they are required to speak on the phone with a distraught customer. If you hire extraordinary people, and commit to investment in their development, they will enjoy their job and be prepared to go the extra mile.'

In the computer networks world, 'the last mile' is the term given to the local phone connection – a bottleneck impeding the growth of the connected business world that is now being replaced by broadband solutions. But from the service-oriented viewpoint that rules at Rackspace, the last mile is the extra mile its team will run to ensure the company's customers continue to experience excellence. And this is the mile that counts.

Chapter 3

Operational effectiveness

Introduction

Research into long-term, successful buyer–seller relationships from Cranfield School of Management demonstrates that customers continue to turn to particular companies because they are easy to do business with. The roles of quality, technical know-how, price and other features take second place to the desire for error-free transactions. For organisations, achieving this means creating their value offering around an understanding of exactly what it is customers' desire. This understanding then forms the focus of the organisation's activities. In many respects, it means turning the supply chain on its head and thinking about taking the customer as the point of departure for the organisation, and not its final destination. Making this an operational reality is then dependent on the effectiveness of service delivery processes and programmes.

In essence, organisations aim to deliver the 'perfect customer experience'. This concept is a valuable one in focusing the resources of the organisation. One of the best examples of its use is by Guinness in the mid-1990s who based an overhaul of their business processes on insight generated into what customers wanted from the company. This was expressed as the 'perfect pint in every pub' and was used to inform internal decision-making about which processes needed to be in place to ensure consistent delivery of the perfect pint, enabling them to adopt a cross-functional approach to business. Guinness worked with its partners in the supply chain to educate the pub trade about the importance of looking after the product and serving it correctly. Consumers were also targeted with award winning advertising that extolled the virtues of waiting for the perfect pint. This co-ordinated range of activities, based on a clear strategy, propelled Guinness to achieve its highest ever share of the total draught market.

Delivering this 'perfect customer experience' is not, however, a one off event. Organisations that galvanise the business behind the concept for a short period only will quickly find themselves falling back into a less effective, production-driven approach to service excellence. To overcome this risk, it is important that service delivery processes and programmes are subject to continuous improvement. Many organisations ensure this happens by adopting one or more techniques, including Six Sigma and benchmarking, both of which are discussed below. Best practice organisations go one stage further and are able to track the cost of servicing a single transaction and many also track the costs of non-conformance. These are the costs incurred when the organisation fails to do things right first time. These may include costs of rework, administering complaints or discounts or refunds to customers.

Organisational effectiveness makes up the second vector in the Service Excellence model. It is often underplayed by many organisations entering the Awards, which is surprising given its influential role in service delivery.

This chapter

This chapter therefore focuses on operational effectiveness and breaks it down into its constituent elements. These are discussed around the series of statements that make up this section of the Service Excellence Awards self-assessment questionnaire:

- Customers consider us easy to do business with.
- We enhance business performance through continuous improvement.
- We can deal equally effectively with customers over multiple channels.
- We deal with service failures effectively.
- We use the web to enhance the customer's experience.

These elements are considered in turn and then best practice is illustrated through the cases of two Awards winners: TNT (from the business-to-business sector) and the Dental Practice Board (from public services).

Customers consider us easy to do business with

Being easy to do business with, regardless of industry sector, brings rich rewards as customers not only comment on the ease and efficiency of business systems and processes, but are also prepared to pay a premium price because of the quality of the customer experience. They make this judgement on the basis of access to information, simplicity and the friendliness of systems and procedures, as well as the willingness of the organisation to make life easy for customers. All of this is predicated on a profound understanding of the value that customers seek. This can best be expressed in terms of the four Cs: customer needs and wants, convenience factors, costs (and not just the monetary value but also aspects such as cognitive effort, time spent travelling, etc.) and communication. The latter refers to how the customer wishes to be communicated with. Some customers are happy for organisations to use their personal details quite freely while others prefer them to keep their distance.

Best practice organisations are responsive to customers and their processes and procedures give the impression of an almost intuitive organisation. This is where managers and frontline staff appear to perceive the truth of things without reasoning or analysis. They are able to put themselves in the customer's shoes and see the benefit of taking a particular course of action without needing any rational validation. When this approach is embedded in processes that empower staff to deal with customers in an individual way, then levels of customer satisfaction rise. Tesco, for example, empowers staff to respond to legitimate customer complaints by giving them the authority to replace products or issue reimbursements without having to refer to supervisors. In doing so, the company demonstrates a respect for their employees' ability to assess situations and manage customer relations. Customers, in turn, are made to feel valued and respected.

Where organisations are able to build a business model around the insights they have into what it takes to be easy to do business with, they are then in a position to change the rules of the marketplace. Understanding these key criteria enables them to redefine the customer needs the industry is focusing on. Virgin Group is one such organisation that has demonstrated time and again how to bring radically new products and services into the marketplace without necessarily being the first to market in a particular sector. For example, Awards winners Virgin One made it easier for customers to manage all their finances, including mortgages, savings and income from a single account and Virgin Mobile (who have also been Awards winners) offered customers a single, simple tariff when other operators were confronting customers with an array of complicated tariffs. Professors Kim and Mauborgne, from the French business school Insead, use the term 'value innovators' to describe organisations that adopt these sorts of approaches to business. In effect, the competition is left standing as old sources of advantage are destroyed and new ones created.

We enhance business performance through continuous improvement

Ensuring that the 'perfect customer experience' is delivered every time is dependent on the processes and practices in place within the organisation. And these, in turn, are optimised through an environment of continuous improvement, where managers encourage their staff to identify and improve product and service delivery. Where performance improvement is an ad hoc activity, organisations find it difficult to maintain consistency, giving rise to variable levels of customer service. In best practice organisations, organisation wide, data driven continuous improvement leads to improved business results.

To achieve this operational effectiveness, organisations use a number of methods, where implementation is supported with formal tools and techniques. These may include benchmarking, either internally, within a particular industry or across industries. Or there may be some other form of process control, such as working to the ISO 9000 series of quality standards that take a Plan-Do-Check-Act approach, or a method such as Six Sigma.

Six Sigma has become the focus of much managerial interest in recent years but has, in fact, been around since the 1930s. The techniques underpinning the approach currently associated with GE were first developed by William Shewart before the Second World War and have been applied in the manufacturing sector since then. Motorola was the company that first developed the Six Sigma methodology in the 1980s and it was GE, under the leadership of Jack Welch, who evolved the process. They claim to have realised savings of over $1.5 billion net of the investments made. Perhaps unsurprisingly, other kinds of organisation are now taking an interest in this methodology and applying it.

Six Sigma is a management philosophy that emphasises extremely high objectives, collecting data and analysing results to a fine degree as a way to reduce defects in products and services. The Greek letter *sigma* is sometimes used to denote variation from a standard. The philosophy behind Six Sigma is that if you measure how many defects are in a process, then you can figure out how to systematically eliminate them and get as close to perfection as possible. In order for a company to achieve Six Sigma, it cannot produce more than 3.4 defects per million occurrences.

In essence, this approach serves to define the boundaries of acceptability between error-free and non-compliant transactions. Six Sigma methods are typically implemented through a process that embraces senior management support, the training of statistical process management specialists, the identification of initial and subsequent projects, and the measurement of the process. Projects are driven by teams through a process known as DMAIC (define, measure, analyse, improve and control). The important issue in all of this is that the organisation should work to balance its focus on internal and external events. It is all too easy for an organisation to become very inward looking when seeking to implement a method such as Six Sigma and to fail to keep up with changing customer demands. One of the advantages of a scheme such as the Service Excellence Awards is that the emphasis of each of the five vectors provides senior managers with a balanced approach to business development.

We can deal equally effectively with customers over multiple channels

One of the key drivers of the changing marketplace is the current proliferation of media and channels. This opens up new opportunities for organisations as well as customers. Some organisations are choosing to cut out traditional media and channels from their approach to delivering service excellence, while others are using them to complement their existing portfolio. However, regardless of which business model is followed, it is obvious that developments across the board are putting the customer more firmly into the driving seat and organisations need to respond to this.

The role of both media and channels is of vital importance in operational effectiveness as it relates to how and where the exchange of value between the customer and the organisation takes place. Media strategies have to do with how the value proposition is communicated, while channel strategies have to do with how it is transacted. In the era of mass marketing, media and channels were distinguishable from one another and were managed as stand alone entities. For example, television was considered a medium and retail was a channel. Today, media and channels have become closely related and even interchangeable. Where dialogue can take place, so the option to transact also arises. The challenge for managers is to devise strategies that embrace convergence with the aim of developing superior levels of customer responsiveness.

Making the most of connectivity has both an internal and an external component. Internally, the goal is to generate data across the various media and channels to create a single, unified view of the customer. This single view ensures that, regardless of the medium or channel through which the customer interacts with the organisation, the customer is recognised and the history of their relationship is remembered. Achieving this single view is dependent on having clear objectives in place for the management of data.

Externally, on the other hand, organisations aim to replicate the experience of a one-to-one relationship where the customer feels they are being spoken to by the same person in every encounter. This may well be despite the fact that an organisation will use many individuals to fulfil this task, and often through multi-channel call centres.

When call centres first appeared in the UK they were held up to be the future of customer service. By offering a central point of customer contact, the call centre was seen as the answer to a comprehensive approach to customer service. Today, these are big business, with an estimated 6000 call centres in Britain and the number expected to rise to 8000 by 2005. The UK industry now employs almost 500,000 people, or 1.7 per cent of the working population. However laudable and popular an idea, the call centre's reputation has been tarnished over time due to adverse publicity and dreadful customer experiences. In too many cases these centres have been exposed as a means of cutting costs rather than improving service levels. Some organisations, however, go to great lengths to make their call centres as 'human' and customer-friendly as possible. Awards winner Virgin Mobile's call centre is located at its headquarters in Wiltshire. The centre is light, airy and divided into sections staffed by different teams that work in light-hearted competition with each other. This pleasant working environment helps keep staff motivation high, and this in turn has a positive impact on customer satisfaction.

We deal with service failures effectively

As discussed in Chapter 1, most dissatisfied customers do not complain to companies when they receive poor service, they just do not return in the future. However for those who do complain, the way the company manages that complaint is a vital ingredient in managing service excellence. There are a number of key aspects to managing service failures effectively.

First, speed of response to customer complaints is particularly important. If a complaint can be resolved quickly and effectively, then customers will generally be satisfied. Unfortunately, research shows that only six per cent of customers receive such an immediate response. Most customers have to wait for a response, which then drives up the costs for business, as well as the dissatisfaction for the customer (Figure 3.1).

Secondly, if a complaint can be resolved quickly, then the chances are that customers can be retained by the business depending on whether or not it is a major or minor complaint. If, however, the complaint is not resolved then the chances of a customer buying again decreases dramatically to 19 per cent for major complaints and 46 per cent for minor complaints (Figure 3.2).

Thirdly, the extent to which staff are trained to deal with service failures can have a dramatic impact on customer satisfaction. In service excellence companies, staff are often provided with a lot of training in dealing with customers complaints. In Virgin One for example staff are empowered to do whatever they feel is necessary

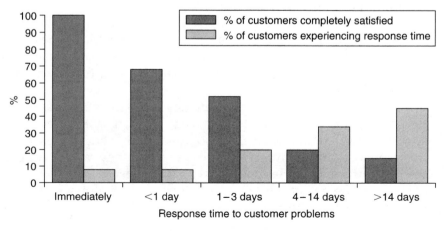

Figure 3.1 Response time impact on customer satisfaction

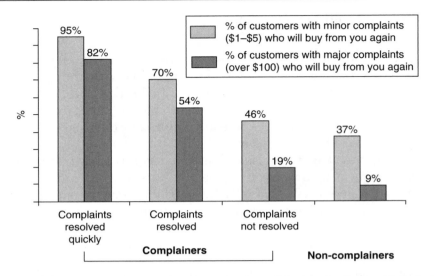

Figure 3.2 The percentage of customers who will buy again. *Source:* Technical Assisted Research Programme

to solve particular problems. This may take the form of compensation or suitable gifts to a particular value. However, it may also include being sympathetic to a particular dilemma that the customer faces through no fault of their own. Staff are encouraged to use their initiative and judgement in dealing with complaints, shying away from prescribed remedies that become mechanical and transparent to the customer.

Fourthly, excellent companies are able to learn from their service failures and put practices and procedures in place to avoid such pitfalls in the future. They are not afraid of change and are happy to revisit processes that can enhance service excellence. These companies see service failures as opportunities, not threats. Complaints are welcomed with open arms as a mechanism for process improvements not as something to be hidden from view.

Finally, many of the service excellence companies also use market research techniques to try to uncover service failures. As well as survey-based techniques, many also use mystery shopper research to try to identify failures in service delivery so that they can be addressed before they damage relationships with their customers.

Dealing effectively with service failure is the hallmark of a truly customer-centric company. Research shows that companies that do this well are able to develop even better relationships with their customers, than if their customers had never experienced service failure in the first place. The rationale behind this is that once a customer experiences service failure and a company responds well to that failure, customers are then able to relax in the knowledge that if things go wrong the company will be able to sort it out.

We use the web to enhance the customer's experience

Many organisations are restructuring their operations to provide electronic-based services for their customers, their employees and in some cases, for their suppliers. Electronic commerce (e-commerce) is challenging traditional business models and creating new ways of accessing customers that simultaneously gives customers more control in the exchange process. Information and services offered become more transparent as customers find they can order what they want, how and when they want – all at the click of a button.

Web-based organisations, either 'brick' (bricks and mortar businesses with additional web channels) or 'click' (Internet only organisations), have created multi-million pound industries providing instant, innovative, customer-controlled competition for traditional service providers. This can only increase in intensity as e-commerce further penetrates business and personal life. The challenge for organisations is to understand how best to utilise this medium.

The term 'e-service' is used to describe the delivery of service using new media such as PCs but also via other technologies such as digital TV, mobile phones and personal digital assistants (PDAs). E-services exist across most of the service sector: banking, retailing, airlines, information and utilities. For consumers this means greater choice, shopping and information from home or office while for business-to-business customers, it will mean a more transparent market with transparent pricing, accessibility to more suppliers, the capability to track deliveries and the ability to undertake electronic trading such as web-based purchase orders, invoices and payments.

As operations management academics Robert Johnston and Graham Clark point out, the principal advantages for service providers are that: customers can have immediate access – they can visit web sites at any time of day, meaning that organisations can provide services 24 hours a day; local businesses have the opportunity to become global; the web opens up additional opportunities to build brands as customers will form an impression of an organisation from its web site activities; customers gain more control over the purchase process; information can be made available to customers that would previously have been uneconomical; and opportunities exist to link web sites of a complementary nature. Service Excellence Awards winners demonstrate a number of ways in which these benefits can be used as an effective means of delighting customers.

Rackspace Managed Hosting (featured in Chapter 1), for example, has a proactive chat facility on its web site that connects visitors directly to a Rackspace team member, meaning that Rackspace customers and prospects can interact in an unstructured way, using informal language and without having to navigate the company's site. This provides a powerful human dimension to the web-based interaction. Alternatively, the Veterans Agency (presented later in Chapter 6) uses its web site to focus attention on its key performance indicators and regularly updates these to keep the public informed of how well it is doing.

Summary points

- Successful, long-term business relationships are underscored by a compelling premise that customers find the organisation easy to do business with.
- Organisations that are easy to do business with stay close to customers and their changing demands. They think in terms of the four Cs (customer needs and wants, cost, convenience and communication), rather than the four Ps (product, price, place and promotion).
- Organisational effectiveness is best demonstrated where employees are empowered to deal with customers on what may appear to be an intuitive basis.
- Best practice organisations adopt continuous, organisation wide, data-driven processes of improvement and use various methods, tools and techniques to ensure error-free transactions.
- The goal of a multimedia/multi-channel strategy is to ensure that the customer has a perfect experience across all the media and channels used. Each time the customer comes into contact with an organisation, they should feel like they are talking to the same person.
- How companies deal with service failures is a vital ingredient in managing service excellence. Speed of response, training, learning from service failures as well as market research techniques are all valuable tools in the quest for service excellence.

- The web can be used to great advantage in enhancing the customer's service experience, providing the organisation has a deep understanding of how the value offering can be most effectively augmented through this channel.

Further reading

Robert Johnston and Graham Clark (2001). *Service Operations Management*. FT Prentice Hall.
Zeithaml, V.A., Parasuranam, A. and Berry, L.L. (1990). *Delivering Quality Service*. Free Press.
Susan Baker (2003). *New Consumer Marketing*. Wiley.

Best practice cases

Introduction

It has been said of the first best practice case in this chapter, that if service excellence is viewed as a journey, then the vehicle in front most likely has TNT Express Services emblazoned on its sides. TNT was named Overall and Business-to-Business Award winners in 2000, a year that saw their business go from strength to strength. Revenues had shown an increase well in excess of the market norm and to support customer service during this period, the company introduced a number of innovations ranging from an Expressing Excellence Workout quality programme, to new technology, such as radio frequency scanning and mobile data transfer between depots and vehicles. These tools and techniques were introduced as a means of ensuring the company maintains a continuous approach to quality improvement.

As part of TNT's integrated approach to service excellence, key performance indicators (KPIs) and internal marketing activities also play a role. For example, internal marketing activities are routinely focused on the attainment of particular performance targets and efforts are made to ensure that all employees understand the importance of specific initiatives. A further secret of TNT's success is down to the way in which it works with customers as the source of all insight into how to improve their service offering. TNT was a popular winner amongst the other finalists in 2000 and aspects of its approach are still talked about by Service Excellence Awards judges today.

The second case study illustrating operational effectiveness is drawn from the public services sector of Awards winners, the Dental Practice Board. Their business could not be more different. Within the National Health Service the Board performs a very important dual role – on the one hand, it is responsible for paying dentists promptly and accurately and on the other, it is charged with protecting the interests of patients, dentists and taxpayers through stringent financial and quality checks. The Board also promotes a wider knowledge of dental care and serves the needs of policy makers and other health authorities. While many organisations would stall in the face of this level of complexity, the Dental Practice Board exceeds expectations.

Its success is founded on the clear vision and leadership skills of its CEO, John Taylor, who brings to the post years of private sector experience. His clarity and commitment are echoed in the passion for continuous improvement that is shown by the Board's staff. The organisation employs a mix of public and professional standards as a means of maintaining its focus on operational issues, as the case study demonstrates.

a ᏜTPG company

TNT Express Services UK & Ireland

Introduction

TNT Express Services' 9,000 employees deliver approximately 42 million items on behalf of business customers every year. Operating out of more than 70 locations in the UK and Ireland, TNT's 3500 vehicles are a vital part of the business-to-business scene. The company's sales were £650 million in 2002 – a figure that reflected the success of TNT's strategy to double the value of the business over a five-year period from 1997. In a very crowded and ultra competitive market, much of TNT's consistent success can be traced to its commitment to innovation, quality and continuous improvement.

Maintaining an innovative approach

TNT Express Services has been consistently out in front since it revolutionised the UK parcels business in 1980 with its TNT Overnite service. There was no nationwide overnight delivery service available to British business customers before, and none of the delivery companies had the technology to enable communications with drivers on the road. The company's history since those early days is studded with innovation milestones. TNT's business is built on speed, efficiency and the ability to improve its delivery capabilities on a continuous basis. At TNT, every activity is geared towards making the business run better on behalf of its customers.

TNT has solved the lurking paradox of continuous improvement: how to make improvement a part of day-to-day activities, yet keep it prominent as a focus of attention. Quality programmes can easily become tired with repetition. The company recognised this danger early on when its original quality circles did not seem to be producing the results everyone wanted. The circle meetings had become long-winded, unfocused – and boring. TNT found a new model to replace the quality circles: the Expressing Excellence Workout. According to Nigel Barton, Operations Director at TNT, 'we stole the idea with pride from BancOne.' The company had encountered the US retail bank on a service study tour, and been impressed with the highly focused and results-oriented flavour of the bank's quality programme. TNT took the programme and changed it to fit the company's specific needs.

Each Expressing Excellence Workout lasts four or five hours. The session has a defined mission, and a dedicated facilitator. The aim is to attack the subject in depth and at speed, and to implement changes as a result. In the first wave of Workouts, the company tackled ways of improving its delivery-on-time rate. These events led to company-wide operational changes to improve performance.

The second wave of Workout sessions enabled local teams to tackle local issues. TNT is a distributed company, with staff at its network of 63 sites working collaboratively to keep deliveries moving. With help from the Workout methodology's originators at consultants KPMG, TNT trained each of its general managers to facilitate sessions. For the locally focused Workouts, facilitators were assigned away from their home depots to ensure objectivity.

The Expressing Excellence Workout is a classic example of how successful organisations take working models from outside the company and optimise them for their own purposes and goals. The broad-brush concept of quality circles proved a bad fit with TNT's culture and timescales. The more directed, problem-solving style of the Workout keeps the team trained on the target of improved service. It also demands practicable outputs: items for action that can be implemented immediately, with immediate beneficial impact on the business. With a delivery business striving to beat delays in its physical channels, TNT needs tools for improving operational excellence that can be folded into day-to-day operations without causing loss or degradation in its services. Expressing Excellence lets the company make modifications to its business in-flight.

A practical improvement programme designed for the business is a key element in ensuring continued operational excellence, but even the best designed programme can become stale. TNT guards against this danger by redressing its improvement efforts to keep them fresh. In 2003, for example, each manager was tasked with a specific area for improvement for implementation at mid-year. The initiatives were monitored closely over the second half of the year, and judged at year-end. The winner received a trip to Johannesburg in the depths of the British winter.

Lessons learned

TNT's experience with running quality improvement programmes has revealed two truths about their business that also apply to many other organisations. The first is that improvements in some processes are limited by the available technologies. As Barton says, there comes a point where 'better management' refuses to yield any further benefits. At this point, the team may have to consider changing the process to take advantage of an emerging technology that will enable a new way of working. Such transitions carry their own risks. However, these risks can often be mitigated by importing the experience and practices of earlier adopters in other fields, much as TNT did with its adaptations for the Expressing Excellence Workout.

The second fundamental lesson that emerges from TNT's experience is the relationship between national, or company-wide, issues and local issues. For TNT, the connection between national practice and local delivery should be seamless: after all, the company exists to move physical items to specified locations. It is in the business of being instantaneously ubiquitous – a national force with infinitely local presence. Yet the local and national levels of operation generate different concerns, and often require different types of solution. National practice and policy provides a degree of standardisation that ensures local teams are working with the best tools and techniques the company can devise.

However, national attention cannot eradicate local obstructions or irritants. The Expressing Excellence Workout lets local teams tackle the issues in their immediate environment without reference to national authority. At the same time, local teams can tag 'points of pain' that they have identified in operational processes and promote them to the national level for consideration as generic issues. Sometimes ideas generated at the local level cannot be implemented as company-wide practices, often because of legal constraints that are not immediately obvious at the customer interface. However, the constant questioning of practices and processes is at the heart of the organisation's quality approach. There are no 'no-go' areas.

Expressing Excellence and other tools

The Expressing Excellence programme has now been in operation for ten years. The programme's objectives have remained constant throughout that time. They aim to:

- improve service quality and provide outstanding customer satisfaction;
- operate clear customer care policies soundly based on market research;
- continuously communicate and implement improved customer care techniques.

The programme's effectiveness is measured according to the following customer satisfaction outcomes, which are shared throughout the company:

- retain clients and increase the number of customers trading every week;
- improve the percentage of deliveries made on time;
- reduce the number of linehaul (long distance) vehicles arriving after scheduled arrival times at hub depots;
- decrease the value and number of credit notes issued;
- reduce customer claims in number and as a percentage of revenue;
- decrease the number of outstanding invoice queries at the end of each week;

- increase the frequency of contacts with existing and prospective customers;
- improve telephone response times.

The company's success in the last area was noted in the consumer magazine *Which?*: 'If you want to know how to answer the telephone, ring TNT.'

Expressing Excellence is a prominent feature of TNT's quality mission, but it is complemented by a range of further tools, channels and incentive schemes. Regular Talkback sessions enable team members to raise issues and challenge work methods outside of the Workout programme. These sessions ensure a constant dialogue centred on operational excellence. The company also runs a scheme called Opportunities for Improvement that allows team members to post ideas for consideration. For people who feel nervous taking part in group discussions, or who prefer to hone their ideas on paper, the scheme is an ideal channel for their creativity. Barton receives an average of one idea every day through this route.

Continuous improvement is further institutionalised through TNT's Academies. Each unit has an Academy that exists to facilitate and co-ordinate distance learning, and provide other resources for team members to improve their knowledge and skills. Achievement in the Academies is recognised by the company and cash awards are made for success in exams. Those Academies focused on customer service and operational excellence are the most popular of a well-supported and well-attended set of Academy offerings.

Making process improvements

TNT's examples of process improvement sound a common theme: a direct connection between personal observation in the field, and systemic changes to organisational practices. For example, team members in the customer services function used to grapple with complex customs laws affecting different territories, striving to clarify the legal path for deliveries while talking with customers. This was information that remained outside the traditional boundary of customer relationship management (CRM) systems, which are naturally designed around customer information. The team asked for a solution that they could click on, as a replacement for the manual Rolodex they had to consult. The company built a searchable database for the team, known fondly as 'the oracle'. The system is linked into the CRM environment, and offers field-sensitive help. This means that if a customer services agent is using the 'dangerous goods' field, for example, the knowledge base will produce the relevant customs information on the screen alongside the field. TNT's 'oracle' effectively aggregates customs information with knowledge about where it needs to be applied within the business process. It saves time – and potentially costly errors.

Another example of successful process improvement at TNT shows that people can be not only initiators of new practices, but also valuable champions of innovations that arise elsewhere in the business environment. TNT had been a pioneer in mobile communications, using technology to speed its delivery process and enable changes to the delivery pattern in real time. During 1994–1995 the organisation began to shift its mobile communications processes from voice-based services to data-enabled solutions. There was a great deal of opposition to this move amongst drivers. The opposition may be hard to credit several years later, when we are used to the proliferation of text messaging by mobile phone and the spread of PDAs (Palm Pilots and the like) amongst mobile workers. Yet the team members were rightly suspicious of a technology that might disrupt their current arrangements and cause them more work. TNT listened to the worries, and ran a pilot project from its Wellingborough depot. Barton was pleasantly taken aback to hear a 10-minute breakdown of how the new system had improved the job – from one of the drivers on the pilot project.

Use of key performance indicators (KPIs)

TNT uses KPIs to formalise management control of the organisation's performance, though Nigel Barton stresses the human dimension of successful KPI use. 'Don't underestimate the time it takes for people to internalise KPIs and use them – and try not to keep changing them,' he advises. The KPI set necessarily evolves, but the company tries to ensure that changes are small and incremental, rather than radical. This is not to suggest that TNT's use of KPIs as a management tool is tentative. In fact, the organisation takes care to integrate its KPI set with all its performance improvement initiatives. For example, whenever the company runs an incentive scheme of any kind, the scheme is related to one or more KPIs so that its effectiveness can be readily measured. TNT is also careful not to let KPIs proliferate and diverge by translation across organisational boundaries. A single KPI may underlie different effects in different areas of the company, but the KPI itself is never compromised.

One four-week campaign serves as an example of how this principle works in practice. This campaign targeted the entry of proof-of-delivery events into the team member's mobile device within a 30-minute window. This goal manifested itself at the operational level as a programme of collectible tee-shirts, where those who collected four shirts would also win a £20 reward. The KPI at the heart of the campaign is not hidden or manipulated, but is linked to a distinctive reward. This ensures that the company's KPIs have continuity and applicability throughout the organisation, with a tight relationship between management intention and operational action.

TNT's lead KPI is on-time delivery, for which it regularly scores 98.5 per cent. This measure incorporates TNT's commitment to flexibility in its delivery service. Last-minute changes to delivery addresses, for example, are not excluded from the events measured to produce this KPI. With high scores like this, TNT must challenge itself to generate new ideas for improvement that are both unique and powerful. One example is the organisation's implementation of the 'proactivity' concept. By 'proactivity' the company means taking service recovery back one step: acting before the customer is even aware of a service failure.

Other leading KPIs include misrouted and missorted consignments; copy consignment notes raised and not matched with original documents; late linehaul (long-distance carrier) services arriving at TNT hubs. Failures to deliver on time are analysed by reason, so that connections with any structural or procedural factors can be made as quickly as possible. Like all good KPI sets, TNT's set is designed to provoke action.

Customers as partners in innovation

TNT's smart use of observation and insight in the field extends quite naturally to its customers. The company regularly involves customers in the development and piloting of new products and services. One example is the TNT Nitebox storage and collection service for field-based engineers, introduced in 2000. The service enables customers to leave items such as urgent spare parts in a network of overnight storage boxes, typically located at petrol stations, for collection by

field-based engineers the following morning. TNT recruited prospective customers to contribute to the design of the service right from the
start. Customers were involved in the design of the collection boxes,
and of the network. The network was partially organised around the
home locations of customers' engineers, making it as convenient as
possible for late drop-offs.

Involving the customers in the creation of the new service allowed
TNT to take advantage of customers' experiences with competing
services and to widen Nitebox's potential user base. The experiences
of customers who had used collection boxes before encouraged the
company to choose more expensive stainless steel for its boxes, rather
than mild steel or aluminium, for reasons of both durability and
appearance. TNT also widened its choice of box sizes from two to four
when prospective customers made it clear that by doing so the company would be able to serve a much wider range of industry users.
The company was also able to build a measure of flexible security into
the offering, so that customers can choose to have a common key for
all its engineers' boxes rather than the standard one key per box. This
detail shows how the organisation can be sensitive to the varying
practices and policies of its customers in the midst of designing a gen-
eralised service.

Involving customers in the design of its products and services
takes TNT's 'proactivity' principle to a supremely high level. Rather
than doing its best to provide what it thinks the market needs, and
then correcting its offerings in the light of measured performance, the
company is striving to roll out products and services that have been
optimised for the customer environment. Variability in customer
requirements is engineered into the offering in the form of options.
The result is a set of offerings that generate few operational exceptions, whose performance is straightforward to monitor, and which
meet a well-defined market need.

Customer involvement is enshrined in the company's practice
of consistently trialling new operational systems with its customers
prior to full rollout. For example, the company introduced a Radio
Frequency Identity (RFID) scanning system in 1999. These intelli-
gent tags, which began appearing on some high-value consumer
goods in 2003, enabled rapid logging and tracking of consignments.
The system has helped to reduce significantly the mis-sorting of
parcels. It was introduced after extensive trials had been undertaken
with a group of major customers to ensure that it would deliver the
expected benefits, and operate effectively with customers' business
processes.

A 'must get through' attitude

TNT Express brings what the company's people call a 'must-get-through' attitude to every activity within the organisation. This deeply ingrained identification of the company's commercial mission with its physical manifestation in the delivery network is the source of TNT's consistently successful engagement with service excellence. There is no disconnect between central management and local service, between KPIs and campaigns, or between the company's offerings and its customers. Operational excellence is visible like a watermark in everything the company does: it is an enduring and endlessly renewed contract of superb service, enacted with pride in every one of its many million transactions.

Dental Practice Board

Introduction

The Dental Practice Board is one of the pivotal but rarely seen organisations that keep the National Health Service (NHS) functioning efficiently. The board is responsible for paying dentists for their NHS work, and also for ensuring quality within the dental service. In effect, the board takes the role of the public's advocate as well as its paymaster. In a mediating role such as this, any inefficiencies stand out with stark clarity.

The board has to act as a frictionless bridge between the country's dentists and patients – and that requires constant and rigorous attention to operational matters. With more than 47 million claims representing £1.5 billion in payments flowing through the organisation every year, processes are targeted for continuous improvement.

The board was born alongside the health service that it serves in 1948. Its mission is to pay dentists promptly and accurately, and to protect the interests of patients, dentists and taxpayers by a painstaking financial and quality audit. On the quality side, the board examines cases relating to around 100,000 patients every year. These examinations split into quality assessment of completed treatments (some 57,000 in 2000/2001) and proposed treatment plans requiring board approval (34,000 in the same period).

The board also has a role in disseminating information about primary dental care, issuing regular guidance publications for policy makers, health authorities and other NHS organisations, dentists and researchers. Its overall budget is around £23 million per year, and it employs nearly 400 people, some 60 of whom are dentists working in the field.

From cost control to a quality focus

Much of the board's success in the area of operational excellence in recent years is attributed to Chief Executive John Taylor, who brought engineering disciplines to an organisation that was heavily paper-bound and short on measures. Taylor insisted that proper tracking of the board's throughput would form the basis of its management and development. This approach was relatively novel in government departments in the early 1990s, so much so that Taylor found himself insisting that the Department of Health give the board performance targets to meet. More than a decade later, targets and service level agreements (SLAs) are firmly embedded in the board's practices and those of the wider department.

Taylor's original remit was to control costs. In common with other organisations, a historic focus on cost control has evolved into a broader concern with quality and value for money. Understanding and capping costs forms the basis for deeper management ambitions: without the basics in place, the organisation's very existence is in jeopardy.

The clearest indicator of the board's success in managing costs is its sevenfold improvement in productivity during the last decade. This has been achieved through relentless pursuit of year-on-year productivity gains of five per cent – a practice more often associated with manufacturing industries than white-collar enterprises.

On a larger timescale, the ratio of staff to documents processed has shrunk to 10 per million from a basis of 87 per million at the board's founding. This translates into a saving for the public purse of over £100 million. This achievement is all the more impressive when we note that the number of claims made annually has risen from eight million to more than 45 million since the board opened for business.

In its quest to control costs, the Dental Practice Board was one of the pioneers of electronic data interchange (EDI), introducing the technology in 1991. Sixty-three per cent of claims are now submitted electronically, cutting down on manual processing and yielding management data as a by-product. Dentists are paid on a four- to five-week schedule, and are given target dates for making their claims. The cycle is therefore self-reinforcing: dentists who meet their claims targets benefit as individuals, and the community as a whole benefits from a more efficient, self-driven system.

Paper claim forms are digitally scanned and the images sent abroad for keying. Outsourcing this part of the claims process is one of the ways that the board has reduced operational costs, and is also an example of how technology can attack stubborn parts of the value chain. When the board first introduced scanners in the mid-1990s the machines were state-of-the-art for their time but still rejected many forms. New scanners with colour and improved resolution are now 'saving' around 500 images per day, considerably improving productivity in this part of the chain.

Best practice standards

Recognising where exceptions can be reengineered into day-to-day processes is a major theme in continuous improvement. Technology is often the key to resolving exceptions on a class basis, but it takes management attention to performance data to reveal where repeated exceptions are forming a pattern. Repeated exceptions have their own costs, but they also create delay in the value chain and therefore erode other elements in the business process.

The board's efficiency statistics are eloquent in themselves, but people form the medium through which service excellence flows. Members of the board's staff show a passion for improvement that translates into a keen interest in adopting standards of best practice from wherever they can find them. The organisation therefore uses public and professional standards as a means of maintaining its vigil on operational issues. It was the first NHS organisation to achieve British Standard BS7799, a set of controls comprising best practices in information security, and it has also achieved ISO 9001 for its quality management system. The board has also achieved British Standards for environment management and complaints management, as well as Investors in People status. According to Taylor:

> If there is a standard that is applicable to our organisation, and can be assessed by an external body, we will consider becoming registered, to continually improve our working practices, promote best practice and demonstrate our status as a world class organisation.

All the standards adopted by the board are consolidated within its evolving integrated management system (IMS). The IMS has developed from the first quality management system introduced in 1993, and now encapsulates the organisation's best-practice-based approach. The system enables the board to target efficiencies and measure progress with tried and tested methodologies. As a result, the organisation can demonstrate reductions such as a halving in general waste and a cut in chemical waste of over 95 per cent to just ten litres per quarter. The board has also been able to decrease its energy usage by 24 per cent through the introduction of initiatives such as eco-friendly lighting and power-saving equipment. These are achievements in areas that without careful planning, control and measurement remain as vague items of concern. Its rigorous approach ensures that the board targets unnecessary costs and removes them from its operational environment – permanently.

This professional approach to standards guides the board's approach to all its responsibilities, not just those that have the clearest mea-surables. The board's duty to prevent and detect fraud and abuse is embodied in its probity assurance management system, an acknow-ledged source of best practice and the most advanced system of its kind in the public sector. The 2001 report on probity assurance was the first comprehensive estimate of improper payments produced by any part of the NHS.

This is typical behaviour in organisations with a well-rooted qual-ity approach: they build explicit systems to meet specific challenges, and strive in each case to demonstrate best practice in each solution. These are solutions that persist in time, yielding benefits on each occasion they are used. Such solutions also travel in business space, delivering working models to colleagues in other organisations with similar goals.

Managing key processes

The board has built a process management system to store its process maps and procedures and guide staff members in their usage. A cycle of 'Plan, Do, Check, Act' underpins all the items in the system, ensuring commonality of approach and continued improvement. The introduction of named process owners, charged with championing improvements to processes at the enterprise level, will further embed the process mindset in the organisation's day-to-day functioning.

Delivering operational excellence at this level requires dedicated team structures as well as supporting systems. The board's commitment to improving its performance is shown in its allocation of human resources to the goal. Team members are appointed to full-time roles in training and facilitation, as well as quality assessment.

The management information that the board generates and uses on a daily basis includes unit costs, operational costs and productivity. All measures in the business are bundled into SLAs, which are built in a hierarchical fashion. There are some 20 or so targets at the top level, where the board negotiates its service level with the Department of Health. These are translated into team-specific targets throughout the organisation, negotiated with the relevant managers. This means that all targets within the business contribute to the board's ultimate contract with the health department, and thereby the general public. Local targets are often promoted upwards through the SLA structure, so that management strategies that are proven in one part of the business are made available elsewhere. Equally, targets can be introduced into SLAs via other stakeholders, including the information needs of other government departments.

The management control structure is therefore subject to constant evolution, with new target areas arriving alongside more mature ones. As Gordon Miles, the board's customer relations manager says, mature targets have their own pressures:

> Once you've reached the Six Sigma level, the challenge is to keep the process at that level. We're processing 47 million transactions a year with 99 per cent of them on time. With that volume, if you take your eye off the ball for a couple of days you can miss the target for the year. You've got to keep managing it on a daily basis.

The importance of culture and structure

Ensuring continuous improvement even in the mature target areas is a matter of organisational culture. Culture provides the day-in, day-out habits of mind that ensure the organisation's attention is trained on the right issues. The board's people naturally look for ways of doing things better. In Miles's phrase, 'we're all looking to iron out wrinkles'.

More formal approaches build on the cultural foundation. Where processes cross major boundaries within the organisation, process management is used to bridge the gap. The board assigns process manager roles that co-exist with the general organisation structure, and pairs up individuals to form living bonds across the departmental divides. This has the further benefit of enabling people from different disciplines to work together, and to appreciate each other's viewpoints and specialisms.

Cross-functional initiatives of this kind also act as a way for the board to model and test new organisational structures. This means that the board is using process management techniques not only to explore and amend its operational effectiveness at the grassroots level, but also as a developmental technique that can inform the evolution of the business as a whole.

Facing new challenges

The Dental Practice Board is faced with the challenges of a changing environment, just as every ambitious organisation is. From October 2005, the system for paying dentists will change radically as primary care trusts begin to commission and pay dentists on a local basis. How the system will work, and how the board's role will be impacted as a result, is currently not clear. For example, the board's role as an assurer of quality within the sector may come to the fore.

In the meantime, the organisation continues to improve its performance while preparing for as many scenarios as it can. It has recognised the key role of primary care trusts in all the scenarios, and is working closely with them on pilot projects. This is an indicator of the board's awareness of structural issues in its market, and the need to plan ahead for changes in its customer relationships.

The board's vision is stated in this way:

In relentless pursuit of improvement we combine public service ethos with commercial sector efficiency and traditional values with modern practice. We aim to be the benchmark for public management.

The connection between 'relentless pursuit' and embodying a benchmark is well made. Through ceaseless attention to operational excellence, the Dental Practice Board has become a model for other public sector organisations – and for any organisation that wants to do more with less, while continuing to press for excellence.

Chapter 4

Engaging people

Introduction

Products and services are increasingly weakly differentiated from each other in the marketplace. You could argue that one bank is much like another and that one washing machine is much like another. Companies can easily copy competitors products and services and in a service industry that is very easily done. Companies can copy other companies' IT systems and they can even copy their customer service strategies. But the one thing that is very difficult to copy, the one thing that can provide companies with a significant competitive advantage, is the quality and history of the relationships that staff have with customers. For this reason, 'engaging people' in the organisation is increasingly becoming a top boardroom agenda item. Companies are recognising that their staff can really add value to customer relationships and as a result are jealously guarding their cultures and their relationships with their staff. They recognise that this is an integral and fundamental part of delivering service excellence to customers. Jeff Bezos, Chief Executive Officer of Amazon.com, echoed this point of view in an interview in the *Wall Street Journal* in July 1999:

> The most important thing we have that's hard to duplicate is our culture of customer obsession. It pervades customer service, logistics, software and marketing. Companies' cultures are impossible to copy. They're like starter pieces of sourdough. Either you've got them or you don't.

Employee behaviour plays a critical role in determining the level of service excellence that is experienced by customers and hence their level of satisfaction with the company, and their willingness to either remain or defect from an organisation. The extent, therefore, to which organisations can attract, keep and motivate quality personnel

will influence their capability to offer quality services to their customers. Consistently offering services that match the requirements of
the external customer will be an important factor in building strong,
long-lasting customer relationships. This chapter, therefore, examines these issues and considers how some of the Service Excellence
Award winners have achieved this; and how they have managed to
create cultures and climates that inspire the hearts and minds of
employees up and down the organisation to deliver great service.

This chapter

This chapter is structured around the five key statements that are
used in the Awards scheme to assess how well companies 'engage'
people in their organisations. These statements are:

- Our people have the right skills and knowledge to perform their
  work well.
- We regularly monitor employee satisfaction and act on the findings.
- We recognise the performance and behaviour of outstanding individuals
  and teams.
- We empower our people to deliver service excellence.
- When recruiting and developing people we focus on attitudes first.

Two previous winners of the Awards scheme have been chosen to
demonstrate how well they have managed to engage their employees in providing service excellence. The companies are: PetCareCo
(Consumer Services) and John Pring & Son (Manufacturing/
Engineering).

Our people have the right skills and knowledge to perform their work well

Having the right skills and knowledge to perform the job well
is the cornerstone to engaging people in a service context. There is
nothing more frustrating for employees than to be thrown in at the
deep end in terms of serving customers and to not know what to do.
Best practice companies adopt two key strategies for ensuring that
their staff are well equipped to do the job. First, they ensure that

they recruit people into the business with the right service attitude. They look for people who are naturally good with customers and care about serving customers well (this is discussed further below). The second strategy is that they ensure that staff receive first class training on how to do their job well. In many service excellence companies this means that they will not be allowed near a customer until they have completed a rigorous induction programme which could last a number of weeks, during which time they will be trained in every aspect of the job and how best to serve customers.

The advantage of adopting such a thorough formal approach is that it makes it abundantly clear to everyone in the organisation what standard of work and behaviour is expected from the start. It leaves little room for 'staff to do their own thing' or even to undermine the company training schemes. However, no matter how well the training is organised and the skills and knowledge to do the job communicated, staff will not excel at their job unless they can work in a culture and climate that fosters service excellence. Many of the best training schemes in the country have failed because returning staff are informed by their colleagues 'not to take any notice of that, that's not how we do things around here!' or 'who do they think they are, we know how to deal with customers and it's not like that!' This is known as 'informal socialisation' and can be very powerful in determining peoples' behaviour when they are at work. It would seem, therefore, that where the successful companies have succeeded is that they have been able to harness 'formal socialisation' through the training programmes and 'informal socialisation' through word of mouth to ensure that they say the same thing. That is, what is preached is actually practised in the organisation and that when staff return from training programmes that enhance their skills and knowledge, they are able to practice their new found skills in an environment that is supportive and helpful.

It is important to remember that there is a real difference between training and learning. Typically, training is measured by testing people, but learning is measured by testing the results of what they do. To learn to do something we must both study and practise. Put another way you can acquire the skills and the knowledge but you have not learned anything until you have put this into practice. This is what 'real' learning is about and this is what the best service excellence companies have achieved. They have recognised that training can only take them so far and that at some point learning must take over. They also recognise that people learn best when they enjoy the learning process and when it is fun. For example, London based, Happy Computers (Overall Award winner and Small Business winner

2003 and Business-to-Business winners 2002) helps 25,000 people a year to develop their skills. Their basic philosophy is that happy people are productive people and their results prove the theory. They ensure that they have bright coloured rooms, flexible times for trainers and even free ice cream for delegates and trainers alike. Staff also receive massages, pedicures and manicures and when the trainers are working away from the centre they don't miss out. Their training packs always contain treats like Jaffa cakes. Happy Computers use their imagination to make training and learning fun; 'Happy' is not just the name of the company, it is the essence of its ethos. The Happy Computers case study is featured in Chapter 5.

We regularly monitor employee satisfaction and act on the findings

'Happy employees equals happy customers' is a phrase that is often quoted, but so often ignored, mainly because it is easy to say but very difficult to achieve. Excellent companies, however, understand the importance of regularly monitoring employee satisfaction. In many ways, they see it as the best indicator of health of the business and the satisfaction of the customers. But why is this the case, why does employee satisfaction play such an important part in customer satisfaction and service excellence? The basic premise to this argument is the acknowledgement that employee satisfaction and employee behaviour plays a critical role in determining the level of service quality that is experienced by customers and hence their level of satisfaction with the company and their willingness to either remain with the company or defect. In labour intensive organisations, the quality of service is determined mostly by the skills and attitude of the people producing the services. All employees are, in fact, part of the process that connects with the customer at the point of sale, or 'moment of truth'. Employees can, therefore, enhance the level of satisfaction customers will experience with a company. Greater customer satisfaction will in turn lead to repeat purchases and positive word-of-mouth communications.

There is much documented evidence that shows that employee satisfaction is strongly correlated with employee performance and in particular with specific facets of performance such as organisational citizenship behaviour, which is behaviour that is not formally required in a job description but is nevertheless critical for organisational success (for example, helping colleagues, volunteering for extra work and so forth). There is also strong support for linkages between employee satisfaction and retention and customer satisfaction and retention. Work undertaken by Bain & Company also suggests a strong link between these two variables. In fact Bain maintains that high customer retention will lead to higher employee satisfaction, as employees will find their job much easier dealing with satisfied customers rather than dissatisfied customers. As a result, employees create a stable and experienced work force that delivers higher service quality at lower cost. This in turn leads to higher customer retention and increased profitability.

Best practice companies use many ways to assess the level of employee satisfaction in their organisations, the most common being questionnaire-based methods. Here confidentiality is assured and transparency of the findings fed back to the employees. Those companies that successfully manage this process make a significant commitment to act on the findings of the reports and if unable to act, explain why. The successful companies are able to point to a history of satisfaction surveys, often completed on a biannual basis, and are able to chart the actions that they have taken as a result of these surveys. Sharing this information with staff highlights the company's commitment to change for the better and as a result staff are more inclined to contribute to further surveys. This creates a positive cycle of success in the organisation which in turn contributes to greater employee and customer satisfaction.

We recognise the performance and behaviour of outstanding individuals and teams

Rewards, recognition and punishments have long been recognised as a means of controlling employees' behaviour and gaining compliance or defiance with respect to management directives. Organisations typically provide their employees with a number of extrinsic and intrinsic rewards. Extrinsic rewards are considered to be the rewards people receive from others; they are provided by external sources such as colleagues, supervisors, managers or the organisation. Extrinsic rewards can include monetary incentives and associated fringe benefits such as cheap loans and company cars. Promotion, recognition and compliments are also considered to be extrinsic rewards. Intrinsic rewards, however, are associated with the job itself and are the positive feelings people derive from the work they do. Intrinsic rewards are self-administered and are based on the personal values of each individual and include, for example, satisfying work, personal responsibility and autonomy. Extrinsic rewards can of course combine with intrinsic rewards to create high levels of motivation and satisfaction for employees and this is a typical feature of many Service Award winners.

The Service Excellence Awards scheme has always tracked and monitored the use of one particular type of extrinsic reward and that is the use of recognition schemes in the companies that enter. This is a powerful way to encourage and motivate the 'right' behaviours among staff. Recognition, as long as it is sincere, can have a really positive effect on people. As well as being motivational, these schemes can also provide an insight into the management style of the business. For example, Chief Executive Alun Jones from TNT sends personalised hand written notes in recognition of staff performance. These schemes do not have to be overly complicated, with lots of form-filling and administration. As the one from TNT shows, some of the best can actually be very simple and straightforward.

As well as recognition schemes, it is also important to consider how best practice companies reward their staff. The purpose of rewarding staff is not just about paying them enough to make them happy or threatening them by cutting their bonus. The main purpose is to use the reward scheme to set personal or team objectives to build or reinforce what the company stands for, to commit to the company's values. So often we see companies where different parts of the business are encouraged to achieve different objectives, that is, the customer service department for customer satisfaction, sales people for sales and so on. However, best practice companies know that this traditional perspective is not viable in the long-term and cannot build relationships with customers who experience the company as a whole. Therefore, if you are serious about building, developing and maintaining long-term profitable relationships with customers, everyone in the organisation must be incentivised to make this happen. The alignment of reward schemes to the values of the business is not only critical to success but can also be used as a mechanism for tracking customer feedback on an ongoing basis.

Another key feature of best practice reward schemes is that the rewards are attainable and relevant. Setting corporate-wide targets may be useful from a chief executive's perspective but if they have no real impact on 'what do I do in my job today', then it is unlikely that the staff will put much effort into achieving them. Similarly if the targets are considered to be 'out of reach', then the staff won't even attempt to meet them. Best practice also means recognising those staff who are not customer facing but who serve those who are. Because of this recognition that 'if you are not serving the customer you are serving someone who is', team-based rewards can be highly beneficial as long as the team ensures that everyone is pulling their weight!

Finally, it is worth commenting on the fact that many best practice companies reward and recognise staff above and beyond standard practice. They will often create ad hoc rewards to recognise occasional exceptional employee behaviour. It may be that a member of staff has excelled in serving a customer or that although they work in a back office job, they have provided excellent internal service which has helped a customer facing employee serve the customer better. In either case it shows that the organisation is taking note. One of the ways many companies do this, is by using customer feedback and input as a way of recognising this kind of exceptional behaviour among staff.

We empower our people to deliver service excellence

One of the most successful aspects of best practice adopted by the winners of the Awards is the empowerment of employees to deliver service excellence. The empowerment and involvement of staff to enable them to use their discretion to deliver a better quality of service to their customers is fundamental to corporate success. There are, however, various types of empowerment available to companies. At one end of the spectrum there is all-out empowerment, where employees have absolute power to do whatever is necessary to satisfy the customer. And at the other end of the spectrum there are milder forms of empowerment, which are basically glorified suggestion schemes. This is where employees can offer suggestions, but the decision-making power rests with the management. There is also 'job empowerment', where jobs are redesigned so that employees can determine how they wish to work and structure their day. The winners of the Service Excellence Awards typically tended to congregate at the upper end of the spectrum, where the employees have more power and discretion to help them in service delivery.

Empowerment means that the company must create the right culture and climate for employees to operate in. For example, employees need to be provided with information about the organisation's performance to enable them to assess the context of their actions. Their rewards should be based on organisational performance and they should be provided with knowledge that enables them to understand and contribute to that organisational performance. Finally, they need to be given the power to take decisions that influence organisational direction and performance. By equipping employees with the appropriate information and training in managing and delivering services, confident staff are better able to provide a faster and more flexible response to customer's needs and to be able to deal with customers in a variety of situations. In fact where service failures do occur, there is evidence that a satisfactorily resolved problem by trained, empowered staff, who take prompt action, may even raise the customer's perception of service quality. Some research has also shown that empowerment can improve employee motivation and job satisfaction, which can lead to improvements in customer satisfaction and customer retention. Although there are significant benefits to empowerment, it should also be remembered that there is an associated cost in terms of labour, recruitment and training costs. Some companies obviously choose to avoid these costs and adopt a more standardised approach to delivering service quality. However, those companies who are Service Excellence Award winners are careful to comment that such costs should be viewed as a longer-term investment in employees and in developing and maintaining long-term trusting relationships with their customers. These companies appreciate how empowerment can affect long-term operational effectiveness (the subject of Chapter 3).

When recruiting and developing people we focus on attitudes first

In recent years many skilled and capable people have been forced back into the job market and it would seem that employers have even greater sources of potential candidates to choose from. The reality, however, is that it is becoming increasingly difficult to find good staff. Skills shortages in key areas mean that employers are often facing the dilemma of trying hard to fill vacancies for some jobs, while at the same time being swamped by floods of applications for other jobs. In our current climate, skill and experience are no longer enough. Employers must also identify those individuals who can contribute to organisational effectiveness and competitive advantage.

In these circumstances good recruitment practices are essential for organisational success, particularly when a company seeks to maintain a culture of service excellence. PetCareCo Ltd and John Pring & Son are examples of companies who owe their success to some extent to the care with which they recruit their employees. However, it should also be remembered that as well as being careful to recruit the best staff, companies also need to be aware that they need to present themselves to would-be employees and influential third-parties as an employer of first choice rather than an employer of last choice. If a company wants to retain talented employees, it must also prove itself to be able to deliver what is promised to prospective employees.

People who staff organisations are the most important single influence in ensuring the future success of the organisation. Interviewers need to be skilled in staff selection and able to detail a person specification which represents the ideal candidate for the job. Organisational criteria and functional/technical criteria should be considered as part of the selection process. Organisational criteria refers to those attributes that an organisation considers valuable in its employees and that affect judgements about a candidate's potential to be successful in an organisation. For example, an organisation may be focused on developing a more customer-oriented culture and wishes to employ people who are warm and friendly and good at communication with customers. Functional/technical criteria refer to specific skills required by departments. For example, a finance department may require candidates to have excellent numeric skills. In a number of the best practice companies it was the organisational criteria that often took precedence above the functional criteria. Many service excellence companies believe that focusing on careful selection of staff is critical if companies are to be successful and gain a competitive advantage. These companies search for individuals whose values and motivation are congruent with the organisation's service ethos. They believe that employee suitability should not necessarily be based on technical skills, which can be taught later, but on psychographic characteristics which show a positive service attitude. For example in Virgin One a typical advert for staff would read 'wanted positive attitude ... with data processing skills'.

Summary points

- Inspiring the hearts and minds of people throughout the organisation to deliver service excellence can provide the company with a competitive advantage that ultimately *cannot* be copied.
- Developing the right skills and knowledge is about moving beyond training to learning, and learning can only be successfully achieved in a culture

which allows staff to enjoy the learning process and to practice in an environment that is helpful and supportive.

- Organisations need to understand that employee satisfaction and employee behaviour play a critical role in determining levels of service quality and customer satisfaction and retention.
- Reward and recognition schemes in organisations need to be aligned to the values of the business in order to encourage and motivate the desired behaviours among staff to achieve organisational success.
- The empowerment of employees is essential for companies wishing to deliver service excellence. But it can only be achieved in an environment that is supportive of empowerment and where staff are provided with the skills and knowledge to be empowered.
- Companies need to carefully select and recruit people whose values and motivations are congruent with their service ethos. Focusing on attitudes first is a key ingredient of success.

Further reading

Benjamin Schneider (ed.) (1990). *Organizational Culture and Climate*. Jossey-Bass.

Helen Peck, Martin Christopher, Adrian Payne and Moira Clark (1999). *Relationship Marketing: Strategy and Implementation* (Text and Cases). London: Butterworth-Heinemann.

Pervaiz Ahmed and Mohammed Rafiq (2002). *Internal Marketing*. Butterworth-Heinemann.

Richard Varey and Barbara Lewis (2000). *Internal Marketing, Directions for Management*. Routledge.

Best practice cases

Introduction

The case studies in this chapter have been chosen for their exemplar best practice in engaging people in their organisations. PetCareCo Ltd (winners of the Consumer Services category in 2001 and 1997 as well as winners of the Small Company Award in 1998 and 1997) is a dedicated chain of one-stop pet care centres that provide accommodation and therapies for dogs, cats and other small animals and birds in one integrated site. The story began when, more than 20 years ago, the founders Anne and Arthur Adlington were about to go on holiday but could not find kennels that they thought were suitable. As a result they decided to set up their own kennels and turn a hobby into a business, but run to professional standards. The case study relates how the company places people at the heart of its business focusing on recruiting the right kind of people who care, and who have the right attitude to deal with the animals as well as their owners. It examines the importance of rewarding and recognising the behaviours that contribute to the company's vision and values, as well as assessing the effectiveness of reward and recognition mechanisms through formal employee satisfaction analysis. Even though the company has grown dramatically over the past few years and is now a joint venture with Mars, PetCareCo is determined that the company's growth must not detract from their philosophy of having genuine people, who want to serve, as the core of their competitive advantage.

The second case focuses on John Pring & Son (winners of the 2002 Manufacturing/Engineering Service Excellence Award), a specialist wire products manufacturer. The case reveals how people are at the heart of the business and that it is people who provide the company with a unique competitive advantage. The case highlights the importance of careful recruitment and ensuring that prospective employees have the right values and attitudes to suit the company. It also examines the role played by the Managing Director, Kevin Croker, in ensuring that his vision for the company is shared with his staff. Honesty and integrity are at the heart of his leadership style, allowing him to involve staff in the business by informing, explaining and discussing the company's performance with them on a regular basis. The case also discusses how John Pring take an active approach to extending the staff's experience outside the factory into their customers' businesses, ensuring that the company maintains a customer-centric orientation. This is also achieved by the company's values which are encapsulated in a set of direct, customer-oriented statements that make up its 'promise' to the customer.

PetCareCo Ltd

Introduction

Chilling out to classical music, catching a video or indulging in some hydrotherapy: it sounds like the perfect holiday. And it is: but the services of PetCareCo are designed for animals, not humans. Each of the company's growing list of centres offers a range of accommodation and therapies for dogs, cats, other small animals and birds – within one integrated site. It's not a dog's life at PetCareCo. The kennels are more properly called apartments: double-glazed and centrally heated, they feature separate rooms for eating and sleeping, and for playing or exercising. There is also an agility area with ramps and tunnels to entertain and exercise the dogs.

Care is central to more than the name of PetCareCo, the world's first and only dedicated chain of one-stop pet care centres. PetCareCo is using the 20 years of experience gained at the luxury Triple 'A' Pet Resort and Care Centre in Boldon near Sunderland to revolutionise the business of looking after owners' precious family pets. A joint venture with Mars, PetCareCo is a marriage of personal vision with professional management.

The company's second site opened at Denton near Manchester in September 2003. The Denton centre includes a large indoor area for pet training, canine hydrotherapy and spa pools, a full-service vet's practice, and training facilities for owners as well as accommodation. At 28,000 square feet, the centre represents an investment of around £3.75 million. A third site is planned for Morley near Leeds in 2004, with many more on the drawing board. The company's pet centres are set to appear at accessible out-of-town sites all over the UK – and beyond – in the years to come.

The importance of people who care

The company needs people who care: who care for animals, and who care about customer experiences. Proudly displayed at their pet care centres is their promise:

Our promise
Our first and only principle is CARE:

- CARE for pets and their owners;
- CARE for our people;
- CARE for the community and the environment.

We are passionate about CARE because:

- CARE is our way of making a difference;
- CARE is catching;
- CARE creates our success.

We pick people who CARE to deliver our promise because:

- CARE means top quality always;
- CARE requires openness;
- CARE demands the highest integrity.

Our promise to you is that we will deliver 'CARE you can touch'. 'This has been a hobbyist industry,' says Sue Sloanes of PetCareCo. 'Traditionally, people with the space and know-how have set up kennels or catteries, while some retailers have tried to add grooming services or veterinarian practices to their stores. But we're leading the industry in creating one-stop centres with broad services and high, consistent quality standards. It's a simple concept really – we're professionalising a cottage industry.'

Sue's job title is 'Talent Scout', a label that reveals the company's approach to recruitment. PetCareCo looks for character as much as skills in the people it hires. The ability to do a specific job within the company is not enough. Team members also need excellent interpersonal skills along with a values-driven ethos. The company also needs openness and honesty in its people, so that it can detect problems and improve the business as rapidly and effectively as possible.

The company realises that knowledge can be added to but that attitudes are incredibly hard to change. By recruiting people who care, PetCareCo ensures that it embeds the right attitudes into its human structure. Many companies claim that they recruit for potential as well as current skills, but the connection with the business's drivers is not always clear. In PetCareCo's case, the growth potential of the business creates a direct link between today's new hires and tomorrow's success. The Denton centre, for example, opened with an establishment of 40 full-time equivalent staff. This complement is expected to scale to 120 within 2 years or so. Multiply this growth curve by the potential roster of UK centres, and the company's staff requirements are high indeed.

The business is organised with a central support team, team leaders and specialists. Specialisms required within the company include groomers and stylists, dog-trainers, and animal behaviourists. All trainers have professional qualifications, and the behaviourists are available to give advice on tackling particular problems. PetCareCo's commitment to future scale means that it is able to recruit for long-term career development. This is a radical departure for the industry, which does not otherwise offer any progression opportunities. Vet nurses, for example, traditionally have little opportunity for promotion or diversification within local veterinarian practices. By working in a team at a PetCareCo centre, a vet nurse has opportunities for development and progression to leadership roles, as well as access to the burgeoning opportunities within the business as it continues to expand.

A personalised service

It is tempting to think that PetCareCo is about pampering its guests and visitors, and services are not cheap compared to traditional suppliers. But the company is keen to stress that what it provides is not luxury, but good care. Team members stand in for pet owners while the pets are in their care, and they apply the same level of personal attention and affection that an owner would. The company's people, therefore, need personality and commitment as well as role-specific skills. This is because PetCareCo's service is a highly personal one. Pet owners regard their pets as members of the family, and seek not only the highest quality of care for them, but also reassurance about the dedication and empathy of the carers. Prospective customers who sense the wrong attitude within a centre will not trust their animals to its care. It is, therefore, vital that every person who might potentially be seen by a customer or impact a customer interaction contributes to the caring feel of the centre. Sue recently ran a recruitment ad for an accountant position with the strapline: 'Can you bring sparkle to accounting and finance?' The company is determined that even the most supposedly non-customer-facing roles be staffed with the same standards as those in the front line. PetCareCo's recruitment process includes three stages. The first two stages are an application form and personal interview. All candidates who pass the interview are invited to an assessment centre event. This event includes team exercises and games that allow the company to find out how an individual ticks, and to see how the chemistry with the company might work.

The challenges of scaling up the business are well understood within PetCareCo. While much of the central support team's day-to-day activity is focused on the myriad tasks associated with creating new sites, there is a keen awareness that the company's growth must not become purely mechanical. 'The larger we get, the more important it is that we have people who are genuine, people who want to serve. We're in the customer service business: the fact that we look after pets is almost the easy bit,' says Sue Sloanes.

Reward and recognition

The reward and recognition programme at PetCareCo is imaginative and tailored to the needs of the business. On top of a basic salary, team members are offered increments linked to the acquisition of new skills outside their existing core competence. This means that as their ability to work in other areas grows, so does their recognised value to the enterprise. Increments are also awarded for qualifications gained, but people must also demonstrate competence in the new qualification within the context of the business. This ensures that all qualifications impact the business in its actual running, and do not become mere paper Awards. The company is proactive in suggesting new areas for personal development and training, and helps team members to grow towards leadership roles.

PetCareCo has thought hard about alternative benefit packages. For example, staff can take up to five weeks leave of absence to undertake voluntary work. The company believes it is important to put something back into the communities it serves. It also recognises that volunteering is an ideal development route, as it introduces people to new situations and ideas that can enrich the company environment. The voluntary work does not have to be related to pets: as long as the scheme is recognised and abides by health and safety regulations, staff may follow any volunteering path.

The company is also introducing an annualised hours scheme that will allow staff to design their own schedules alongside the needs of the business. Team members will be able to take up to 8 weeks off during the year using the scheme. The boarding side of PetCareCo's business is necessarily seasonal, being based around school holidays, so staffing requirements can be complex. Nevertheless the company recognises that flexibility on the part of everyone is the key to ensuring that the enterprise is always able to meet its customer commitments.

PetCareCo uses a form of community recognition and reward scheme that allows people to express their valuation of each other. When the company won its Service Excellence Award in 2001, it was running a successful scheme whereby team members could hand out stars to colleagues, who would wear them on their collars. This scheme has been superseded by a 'Department of the Month' Award and a 'Team Member of the Month' Award for each department, voted for by the staff.

There is also an 'Extra Mile' Award, given to team members who contribute well beyond their normal role. In one case a team member helped a customer who lost a re-homed dog by putting up posters and searching during her own spare time. Another extra-miler noticed that an elderly customer needed help in her home when he picked up her pet, and carried out a list of maintenance tasks for her. These awards help to highlight how the concept of care is closely related to initiative and imagination, as well as the way a caring attitude can reach beyond the boundaries of normal service.

PetCareCo's current reward and recognition strategy is topped off with a Celebration Champion at each centre. The celebration Champion has a budget that can be used to celebrate anything that the team at the centre thinks has contributed to the progress of the business. Celebrations have been run for breaking through customer number targets, achieving set margin levels, and also for outstanding individual contributions. The celebrations involve all the personnel at the site, so that everyone shares in the team's achievement.

Keeping pace with employee feedback

PetCareCo's reward and recognition strategy is designed to support the company's ethos, extending the concept of care into every aspect of the employee relationship. The effectiveness of reward and recognition mechanisms – and other management processes – are monitored through formal employee satisfaction analysis. Employee satisfaction is monitored using a confidential survey. Team members can choose to make their survey returns anonymous, although they can also identify themselves if they want to pursue particular issues. The company has been studying how Microsoft links its employee satisfaction forms back to its business scorecard, and believes that this modification will help to make the exercise more focused and relevant. This formal satisfaction survey is designed very much as a backstop for employee issues. The accent within PetCareCo is on speaking up, and contributing new ideas to the business. Each team has a fortnightly meeting, guided by a six-topic agenda. The agenda includes topics such as what the team has done well in the period, and customer satisfaction levels. The notes from these meetings are posted publicly so that anyone who misses a meeting can catch up.

In alternate weeks, staff members complete 360 degree appraisals of themselves – and of each other. The topics in this tool include challenges faced in the period and how these were overcome. This mechanism could be seen as intrusive or divisive in some organisations, but it has been used at PetCareCo since the beginning of the business and is regarded as a natural activity. The regular team meetings, and culture of openness and honesty, ensure that issues are surfaced and addressed at every opportunity. This allows the appraisal system to be used for purely constructive purposes.

Vision and values

These regular activities take place within a calendar that also includes quarterly Vision Sessions, facilitated by the Managing Director. The primary purpose of these sessions is to remind everyone of the business's mission: 'to change the face of pet care'. The values embodied in the company's promise drive personal training, and are reconfirmed and retold at these events. Vision sessions allow the company's people to remember that 'we aim to change people's lives'. That is a strong statement, but it translates into small – but valuable – practical actions. For example, a centre can invite people in to simply spend time with an animal, because they do not have – or cannot have – any pets of their own. This is a practical instance of vision translating into action. While the Vision Sessions provide a prominent opportunity to discuss the company's mission with the MD, team members know that they can also talk to him at any other time.

Protecting and spreading this strong culture of open communication and practical, vision-based action, is vital to the achievement of PetCareCo's aggressive growth targets. The company is preparing for the day when it has 10 or 20 centres, and must continue to touch the lives of each of its people. Some reassignment of central support duties will allow the core team to continue to address the high-value tasks of maintaining vision and communication, while more mechanical tasks are increasingly formalised and automated.

The challenge of growth also highlights the importance of getting the right split between controlled functional management and individual autonomy. Building a trusted brand implies ensuring consistency as well as quality. Customers need to know that PetCareCo's centres will have the same range and standard of services at any site, just as they expect from a Hilton or Marriott hotel. The company, therefore, recognises that the experiences it creates combine highly defined tasks with the less tangible virtues of good care. It produces and maintains detailed working instructions to ensure that all centres and teams meet quality standards, and it rigorously measures performance against these standards. But nurturing a culture of caring people also implies that well selected – and well motivated – people will want to perform their tasks well. People who care need less supervision, because they also care about the effects of the jobs they are doing. They appreciate the interdependency of roles within the business, and their ultimate impact on the customer experience.

Conclusion

The high rate of repeat business at PetCareCo indicates that the company is getting its caring right. But the company also recognises that it faces little serious competition – yet. What will it do when it has proven its professional, high quality, one-stop centre pet care business model, and helped to create a new industry? The company's people are more than happy to see that day dawn. They believe they are upgrading their industry, and transforming its quality for both customers and employees. This is seen as a responsibility the company holds on behalf of the community. In practical terms, it means that it is happy, for example, to take people and train them for their NVQs and then let them leave if they wish. The company recognises that it may lose some business this way, but feels it is in its best interests to promote the development of the industry as a whole. Companies which define the methods and standards of an industry often retain a senior role as the industry develops, if only because so many professionals pass through its portals. PetCareCo may well become not only the source of a new approach to professional pet care in a new industry, but also the industry's university.

John Pring & Son

Introduction

John Pring & Son operates in a traditional manufacturing industry, yet its attitudes to customer service – and specifically to enabling people – are strikingly modern, as well as being relevant to businesses of all kinds. John Pring makes specialist wire products for applications as diverse as lampshades and cotton baling, using the raw input of – people.

Many companies mouth the mantra that 'our people are our greatest asset' without ever honouring the idea in their day-to-day behaviour, management systems or reward and recognition schemes. At the Sandbach-based John Pring factory, it is immediately obvious that people form the company's winning edge in an industry with tight margins and demanding customers. The maturity of the industry's technologies and supply chains expose the human factor as a key determinant of survival for companies in the sector. Acknowledging that it operates in a commodity market, John Pring has embraced the opportunity to make customer service a premium component of its product. As a result, the company is consistently profitable while its competitors struggle to break even, and it continues to grow its global business.

The company employs 65 people in its Cheshire premises. It has a global customer base, and is also part of USA-based Leggett & Platt, one of the world's largest wire manufacturers and a Fortune 500 company. The team has made a virtue of the constraints imposed by the layout of its factory, which dates back to 1834. A lack of space to hold finished inventory has encouraged John Pring to focus on making products to order with lead times of 7–10 days. The flexibility and responsiveness that this strategy brings is a major factor in its success.

Getting the 'right' people

The company's strong commitment to people starts in its recruitment process. John Pring recognises that the key attributes for success are intrinsic: they are not qualities that can be grafted on to people by training or persuasion. When recruiting, the company looks for the right values and attitudes in terms of enthusiasm, reliability and dedication. Managing Director Kevin Croker believes that if you recruit for these attributes, you can then add role-specific skills through training and experience. This principle applies at all levels of the company, not just staff members on the factory floor.

Focusing on these personal attributes makes the recruitment process more time-consuming and costly than the approach it has replaced. Croker estimates that the previous process resulted in 60 per cent of applicants being offered jobs, whereas the new approach yields only one or two successes for every ten applicants. Any company needs to have the courage of its convictions when switching to a method that seems to give lower and slower results, especially when production is suffering for lack of people. Yet John Pring finds that staff members recruited in the new way are more likely to succeed within the company, and more likely to stay. The recruitment process works as an investment in the future of the company, rather than a short-term solution to immediate gaps.

The change in the recruitment process is based on a belief in the direct connection between people and profitability. John Pring's goal is to be the best supplier for a customer, and the distinguishing factor is not the factory's machines or systems. As Croker says, 'all the *issues* in business track back to people, so the foundations of what we're building is always going to be people.'

Sharing the vision

Walking the talk on valuing people is close to Croker's heart, and key to his success in spreading the concept is his genuine focus on sharing his vision. 'Sharing' is a term that is often abused in business, and sometimes means little more than 'telling'. But Croker takes the trouble to establish common ground among his people, to demonstrate that everyone in the enterprise does have a common interest. He began this process early in his leadership, by calling a full meeting of the whole company. This had never been done before, partly because the value of such an event was not appreciated, and partly because production could not stop to enable a company-wide meeting. Croker arranged the meeting for a Saturday, eating into people's unpaid time – surprising them, but also providing their first clue as to the management's seriousness about the firm's fortunes. Croker challenged everyone to name their reasons for coming to work, and demonstrated how he held exactly the same motivations: to earn a living, to work in a safe and friendly environment, and so on. This was the beginning of a truly shared vision that has continued to grow and consolidate within the company.

Sharing his vision is Croker's strategy for ensuring that his approach lives within the company, rather than being vested solely in himself. The energetic, passionate leader can be a risk factor if the organisation relies on him as its only power source. In this way, John Pring is achieving a culture where customer service, quality and profitability are embedded in the everyday actions of the whole team. Another method that Croker uses to ensure a shared vision is publishing, explaining and discussing the company's performance on a regular basis with the entire staff. Traditionally, there had been a disconnect between the firm's actual business and employees' understanding of their roles and their rewards. Massive contraction within the industry has meant that management cannot insulate the team from market realities, even if it wanted to. There is now a much clearer link between what the company does – and therefore what individuals do – and its overall health. Regular measures of sales and profits against budget are displayed in the factory, as well as production measures such as scrap levels. Croker writes a monthly commentary to explain the data, and to stimulate discussion.

But publishing facts is only part of the communication task: to be meaningful, the traffic has to be two-way. The directors walk the factory floor as often as they can, and encourage queries. Croker admits that in the early days of his new approach the management may have overdone its efforts to communicate, but has since achieved a balance. He is proud that he has business discussions with people on the shop floor that match boardroom discussions for quality, relevance and insight. He has not forgotten his own time as an apprentice, and the institutionalised detachment that used to prevail in industry. The close identification of what people do with how the company performs extends to the company's profit sharing scheme, of which all John Pring's people are members.

Regular face-to-face communication of this kind helps to ensure that the vision is shared throughout the company, and it is crucial that no element of 'spin' creeps in. Croker insists that 'we're all adults, and you should give people the truth'. When tough decisions have to be explained – including the freezing of wages – people may not cheer, but they understand why the decisions have been taken. The inclusive vision ensures that every decision is one that every member of the firm would have taken.

The sense that everyone at John Pring is working for the same ends is enacted in many small but significant ways. For example, in common with other manufacturing businesses, the company receives Christmas gifts from its suppliers. The gifts range from bottles of seasonal cheer to consumer electronics goods. In times gone by these gifts would have been taken home by senior managers. Today's John Pring holds a raffle on the day before the Christmas break. Everyone in the company has a ticket and is assured of a prize – *except* the senior managers. The company also funds a single Christmas party for all of the staff.

Focusing on customers: the promise

As well as working to create and sustain a shared vision within the company, John Pring takes an active approach to extending its people's experience outside the factory and into the concerns of its customers. It has broken with tradition by sending people from all roles to visit customers, rather than just sales staff or technical specialists. A rolling programme ensures that everyone will have an opportunity to make such a visit. The company recently sent a staff member to Australia – the destination that workers joked would never be the target for a trip. The person who went on the trip returned with a new store of technical knowledge, customer insight and infectious enthusiasm. Sending people out to customers has never been done in John Pring's industry, but the benefits are enormous. People who make wire for, say, a coat-hanger manufacturer now know the people who make the coat-hangers, and have discussed ways that the wire product can be improved for their usage. The effects on customer retention and satisfaction are enormous. Organising and supporting the visits is expensive; but, like the recruitment process, it makes for a compelling investment in the well-being of the company.

It is this very practical and embedded people orientation that makes John Pring special. The close connection between what people do, and the success of the business, is part of the behavioural fabric of the business. As Kevin Croker says, 'it's not a "job", it's a way of life'. For habits of excellence to permeate the daily life of an organisation, the values by which people select and judge their behaviours must be clear and memorable. John Pring's values are encapsulated in a set of direct, customer-oriented statements that make up its 'promise':

- We will always aim to meet the shortest possible delivery times.
- We will respond to our customers' needs in a fast, efficient and courteous manner.
- We will always provide the best value for money wire products available.
- We will always respond to queries within one hour.
- We will provide full documentation, certification and records for all delivered goods.
- We will only use the best quality raw materials for our products.
- We will check that you are satisfied with our work.
- We will give you one contact person for any account queries – and resolve them within five working days.
- We will provide technical advice and support.
- We will deliver the most cost effective solution.
- We will guarantee all of our work and products.

These strong statements form a kind of cultural contract, or constitution, within the organisation. They also place the emphasis for people's activities on positive customer benefits, providing a balance to potentially negative drivers such as industry contraction. As expressions of 'the way of life' at John Pring, the elements of the company's promise help to transfer management goals to the individual care of the people who must achieve them.

Achievement is recognised within the company using both formal and informal methods, in another demonstration of its holistic approach to enablement. The annual conference includes a session where the company recognises achievements of all kinds, from attendance records to long service awards, as well as outstanding performance. But the company also gives impromptu awards throughout the year, showing that it always has the time – and attention – to recognise excellence.

A learning organisation

John Pring's experience with the Service Excellence Awards provides an example of people enablement in its own right. Like many companies, John Pring has used the Awards process as a way of learning about best practice and benchmarking itself against other organisations. The company has participated in the Awards for seven years, using the process as a means of examining its own performance, and acting on the panel's feedback. This is a further sign that John Pring is a learning organisation: one that seeks to improve its self-knowledge on an ongoing basis. Self-awareness is a fundamental part of any organisation that bases its success on the efforts and beliefs of its people rather than proprietary technology or protected markets. Engaging with external monitors and comparisons, such as those embodied in the Service Excellence Awards, can provide both reflectivity and inspiration.

For example, the team at John Pring based part of their 2002 entry on feedback provided by the panel in its 2001 benchmark report. The two issues highlighted in the report were the cascading of information throughout the company in an effective manner, and continued improvements in operational control. The company addressed the communications issues through a range of channels including briefing sessions, union routes and training sessions. The company also implemented a full appraisal system for all its staff, including training for the appraisers prior to the system's first run. At the same time it used its pursuit of the ISO 9001:2000 Standard to drive operational improvements, achieving accreditation in February 2002.

John Pring's belief in the Awards process as an influence on its business success has made it a passionate advocate of the scheme. The company's assessment of the benefits of participation has led it to share its experiences with other companies via organisations such as the Chamber of Commerce, Enterprise Council and TEC International. The company has also detailed its experiences for the ISTC union's leadership and its 40,000 members via the union's magazine. This urge to share what it has learned demonstrates how John Pring's belief in enabling people extends beyond the boundaries of its organisation to the wider commercial environment.

Conclusion

In the final analysis, John Pring's continuing commercial success relies on its being able to sell on service and quality, not price. Service and quality are attributes that can only be created and delivered through people. No amount of branding gloss or bought-in wisdom can replace the positive motivation of knowledgeable, customer-oriented people. John Pring supplies technical back-up to all its customers as a standard component of its offering. Technical advice extends to the pre-sales period, where the company uses a consultative approach to, for example, establishing the product and quantity required to meet a customer's requirements. The aim is to build genuine partnerships with customers, so that supplier and customer are working together to meet needs. When a problem does arise after a sale has been made, the company reacts promptly, often sending a technical expert from the production department to solve the problem at the customer's site. This level of attention, and personal commitment to the customer's success, is more often associated with complex high-tech products and services. John Pring has realised that in today's global and highly competitive markets, no company can afford to regard itself as a commodity supplier. Manufacturers have to wrap products with service: and the only way to do that is to build authentic, empowered teams of committed individuals who believe they can make a positive impact on their customer's lives.

Chapter 5

Leadership and values

Introduction

Leadership and values are the cornerstone of the Service Excellence Awards. They address the direction and culture of the organisation and how successfully the values and leadership of the organisation create a passion for customers. They build a foundation in the business that guides and directs how people behave with each other, what is important and where resources should be focused. Before turning to the questions in this vector of the service excellence questionnaire, it is worth considering leadership and values in turn.

What do we mean by leadership?

There are numerous definitions of leadership and equally many different ways of categorising leadership. Yet despite this, there are very few leaders who really inspire or who can generate the kind of vision and values that are essential for organisational success. Sadly, there are many chief executives and senior managers in business today who are not leaders but good managers and understanding the difference between the two is crucial. Being a manager is a position in the organisation and it comes with power and responsibility, but it does not mean that the position necessarily inspires people to 'follow'. Unless the needs of people within the organisation are taken into account, leadership will be ineffective. People need to give their permission for leaders to lead and have a desire for to follow them.

Leaders need to generate 'followership'. So how can they do that? What are the key elements that form the core of leadership? In their book the 'Essence of Leadership', Professors Andrew and Nada Kakabadse argue that 'the capability to lead must be coupled with the practical skills that leaders need to have to manage their day-to-day affairs'. They have distilled the views of today's great thinkers on leadership and developed a categorisation of leadership, the essence of which is noted here:

- Leadership can be considered to be a special type of power which can command and focus resources to achieve a particular vision, change or goal. Leaders can transform a business by creating a vision of the future, then investing heavily to share that vision with the rest of the organisation.
- Leaders should live the values that they share with the organisation. In other words 'practise what they preach'. Without this, they lack integrity and their 'followership' will disintegrate.
- Leadership involves broad capabilities, including having the skills and ability to handle the mundane, operational and daily transactions of corporate life.
- Leaders need to have a high degree of people skills, to manage the complex human interactions that take place between people to ensure they get the best out of them. They recognise that they need to involve other people to achieve success.
- Leaders need to have good conceptual skills and good judgement to enable them to see opportunities where others are not able to.
- Leaders need to be politically astute. They need to know how to *use* their power in awkward situations and not just to seek power for the sake of it.
- Leadership requires character, namely: ambition, ability, conscience and integrity, so that leaders can follow an ethical and appropriate way forward. Sadly it is these two last aspects of character that are so frequently missing in many leaders, which has led to the recent failures of corporate America.
- Finally, leadership does not necessarily mean that you are the 'boss'. Leadership can be exerted by people who are not in a position of authority.

The importance of values

In his book *The Committed Enterprise*, Professor, consultant and author Hugh Davidson discusses the results of his interviews with 125 organisational leaders on the subject of values. He found that there was broad agreement on three issues in every organisation. Davidson refers to these as the fundamental questions of life and he uses the terms 'purpose' (others may say 'mission'), 'vision' and 'values' to describe them.

- 'Purpose' covers 'What are we here for?'
- 'Vision' handles 'Where are we going?'
- 'Values' answers 'What behaviours will guide us on our journey?'

This chapter focuses on the role of values in the service excellence model. So why are they so important? Put simply, values (sometimes referred to as the 'ethos' of the business or even the 'principles', 'guidelines' or 'rules') are the beliefs that guide our behaviour. They guide everything that happens in an organisation and form the basis on which organisations are founded. Values that are 'lived' in an organisation can be very influential in guiding staff behaviours without having to rely heavily on numerous rules and regulations. Staff know what is expected of them, they know how to behave and how to respond to new or unforeseen circumstances. The stated values in a company are those that are found on posters, mouse mats and are regularly reviewed in staff meetings. Actual values, however, can be observed in the way the organisation works. Successful organisations have only a narrow gap between these two. They work hard to ensure that 'what is preached is practised', and that there is a common understanding in the organisation about what the values mean and how they should be enacted.

Over 90 per cent of the entrants to the Service Excellence Awards have values statements, yet interestingly, one in ten do not include 'customers' in their core values. Only 50 per cent value having 'fun' at work and one quarter do not think 'innovation' is important enough to include as a core value. Eighty per cent of the statements share the four core themes of 'external focus', 'continuous improvement', 'concern for people' and 'social responsibility'. However, recently 'altruism' has appeared as a new emphasis to values. Altruism takes the values of 'concern for people' a stage further to being really concerned about the health, wealth and well-being of people in the organisation. One of the case studies that we will examine in this chapter is CragRats, a Yorkshire-based company specialising in the use of theatre for communication and training for both the public and private sector. They were the Overall and Business-to-Business Winners of the 2001 Service Excellence Awards and are typical of a company that has the value of altruism at the heart of its business. They genuinely care about their employees and help them improve their lives through their relationships with the business. The signs are that 'altruism' will increasingly appear in the value statements of service excellence companies in the future.

This chapter

This chapter is structured around the five key statements that are used in the Awards scheme to assess how well companies achieve leadership and values. These statements are:

- Our values are widely understood and practised.
- Leadership reflects the organisation's values.
- Our processes of management enact our values.
- Senior managers actively champion customers.
- We invest in developing leadership across the organisation.

Two previous winners of the Awards scheme have been chosen to demonstrate how well they have managed to engage their employees in providing service excellence. The companies are: CragRats (Business-to-Business) and Happy Computers (Small Business).

Our values are widely understood and practised

Values are the life blood of the organisation and as a result it is important that they are 'lived' on a daily basis. It is essential that they are widely understood and practised so that they can guide staff behaviour in appropriate ways. However, unfortunately many companies develop values statements and present them to staff without ever having discussed them with the staff. They then wonder why there is a wide gap between stated values and the actual behaviour that people observe in the organisation. It is absolutely vital that draft values are discussed widely with employees and modified in the light of those discussions. Once values are agreed, supporting practices and procedures can then be drawn up to support the values.

A good way of assessing the degree of fit between stated values and actual values is to be a fly on the wall and watch what happens in an organisation. For example, customer focus may be a stated value, but it may be possible to see managers walking past ringing phones and not answering them, or even standing by while a queue of customers wait for service. Another example may be that a company has a stated value around the treatment of employees, yet it may be possible to observe that in a call centre there is nowhere for staff to retreat or relax away from customers. These are exactly the sorts of observations that the judges of the Service Excellence Awards are making when they visit companies. The degree to which the values are 'lived' is constantly assessed, as well as the extent to which they are widely understood and practised. This is why it is important to ensure that values are translated into action. To ensure values really are 'lived', they need to be turned into measurable practices. For example, if a value is to 'identify, anticipate, serve and satisfy customer needs', then one way of measuring this would be to ask when was the last time a particular staff member sat down with a customer to find out their needs. Measuring practices helps focus staff attention on what is important; it guides their behaviour and the future direction of the business.

Leadership reflects the organisation's values

As we have already seen, values are the beliefs that guide our behaviour. In a company, therefore, it is essential that leaders reflect the organisation's values. Without that, the values of the organisation become hollow, empty statements, that are meaningless to staff. At a very senior level in the organisation, if there is a gap between the stated values and the actual values, staff will perceive their leaders not enacting the values of the organisation and will ask themselves why they should do so too. This kind of hypocrisy is endemic in many organisations. There are many companies that have spent vast sums of money on developing values (often with the help of an outside agency), publicising the new values via glossy brochures but never actually manage to change the deep-seated practices that are held at every level in the company. However, if the leaders of the organisation reflect the values and are seen living them on a day-to-day basis then people will take note and realise that the company is serious about what it is trying to achieve. Actions in this respect, speak more powerfully than words as the following quote highlights:

> We judge managers by their actions, not their pious statements of intent.
> Sir Adrian Cadbury

Cascading down values from the top of the organisation is also doomed to failure if there is not a critical mass of support for the values at the top. This support needs to be there before the cascading process starts; otherwise the message will become distorted as it flows throughout the organisation. Conflicts will undoubtedly arise and the power of the values will be diluted. Communication is, therefore, a key ingredient in this cascading process and it is the leader's personal responsibility to get it right. Organisations can communicate in a number of different ways and all of these ways need to be considered when company leaders wish to communicate the values of the organisation both internally and externally. Hugh Davidson has identified eight ways in which companies communicate, and each way should be thought of as an opportunity to reflect the values of the organisation:

1. Actions are the reality of what goes on in an organisation. It is what an organisation does and, as such, provides a very good opportunity to demonstrate organisational values.
2. Behaviour describes how things are done in the organisation and how people treat each other.
3. Face-to-face communication by management includes meetings, presentations, conversations and answers to questions that are posed.
4. Signals are the objects which convey information about an organisation. For example, customer parking taking precedence over executive car parking.
5. The quality and style of the products and services embody the organisation's vision and values. This has the potential to show that the company cares.
6. Advertising, which covers all paid-for communication.
7. Word of mouth and the web are also very important ways for organisations to communicate their values.
8. Comments by other organisations such as the media, government bodies and regulatory bodies, as well as suppliers and competitors.

Our processes of management enact our values

All companies too often spend time and resources on developing values but fail to really embed them into the organisation. In the Service Excellence Awards, the judges seek to examine the extent to which there are systems and processes in place to translate the values of the organisation into strategies and practices, which in turn are linked to managing staff behaviours on a day-to-day basis. Some of the key processes that are considered are as follows:

- The appraisal, promotion and reward schemes are always thoroughly scrutinised to ensure that they are aligned with the values of the organisation. In this context, individuals need to be clear about what their personal objectives are. They should be in line with the organisations' values and should establish what individuals must do and what their individual responsibility is. This guides their behaviour and ensures their own and the company's success. Unfortunately, very often there is a mismatch between the company values and the appraisal and reward scheme. For example, if the staff are appraised and rewarded for customer acquisition but the values of the company are focused on customer satisfaction, staff are likely to be pulled in different directions and may even experience role conflict and ambiguity. The appraisal and reward system should flow from the values of the organisation.
- Organisation structure is also carefully examined as part of the Awards, as it too should be aligned to the organisations' values. For example, if the company values cooperation and teamwork but it is observed that people are working in silos with little opportunity for collaboration, it is likely that the organisation's values will not become embedded in the company.
- How organisations recruit is also a key ingredient in 'fixing' the values in the company. It is important that staff are recruited who are not only attracted by the values of the company, but who are able and capable of enacting those values on a daily basis. If there is a close match between the company and employee values, it is more likely that the staff will be happy and will want to remain with the company.
- It is also important to have mechanisms in place to ensure that the values in a company are continually kept alive. It is very easy to allow values to fade away into the background, especially when times are hard or organisations are experiencing times of stress. Therefore, continually updating practices in line with the values helps to keep them fresh, and building annual themes around specific values can assist in embedding them in the company.

Senior managers actively champion customers

This statement relates to the extent to which senior managers purposefully design a customer-centric organisation and consider customers in their decisions and actions. This is the ideal best practice organisation where 'the customer is king' and where everything from the structure of the organisation to the practices, procedures and rewards are designed and planned with the customer in mind.

The starting point in doing this is always to have a clear vision or picture of where the company wants to go. Good leaders are able to do this. They are able to create a vision of the future and then invest heavily in sharing that vision. Through sharing their vision, they clarify the present and propose future direction, while at the same time inspiring and stimulating people to action. A successful vision should be memorable and clear, and provide a way of generating understanding and commitment from people. As well as being ambitious it should also be customer related and be capable of being translated into measurable strategies. It should also generate debate and, furthermore, invite comment and questions. However, all too often vision statements are uninspiring and bland. They do not paint a picture and, as a result, do not inspire people to follow. Of course when a company is new and is started with a clear vision of what it wants to achieve and how it wants to organise to get there, it is relatively easy to be customer centric. But doing this with an older, more established organisation, which is struggling with legacy systems and power structures that are not customer facing, is an altogether more challenging task. There are examples of both kinds of organisation in this book. In this chapter, for example, we consider CragRats, a company which was founded in 1991 specialising in the use of theatre for communication and training for both the public and private sector. The vision, which inspired the development of the company, was a series of strong value statements, which would become enshrined in the business. In contrast, Nationwide, whose case is explored in the final chapter, shows how an older more established organisation was able to reorient itself around the customer despite the established practices in the company. Again, it did this by having a clear vision and establishing values in the company that everyone could buy into.

We invest in developing leadership across the organisation

As already discussed in Chapter 4, companies who acknowledge that staff can really add value to customer relationships, jealously guard their cultures and relationships with their staff. They recognise that service excellence cannot be bought 'off the shelf', it has to be developed and grown from within. For this reason, best practice companies tend to develop their own leaders. Of all the entrants to the Service

Excellence Awards, 69 per cent of the top teams have come from inside the organisation. TNT refers to this as 'home-grown timber'.

The need to develop leaders across the organisation is now becoming increasingly recognised as essential to corporate success. The key question, though, that all companies are keen to have answered is, 'how do you do it', 'how do you develop leaders?' The recommendations for leadership development are driven by the results of a number of surveys carried at Cranfield School of Management, which highlight ways of developing the actual and latent capacity of individuals. In their book the *Essence of Leadership*, Professors Andrew and Nada Kakabadse particularly emphasise the following:

- *Career development*: Developing leaders through career development helps individuals adopt a wider perspective of their organisation and a positive attitude to relationship management. Giving individuals early exposure to leadership helps them appreciate the challenges of leadership. It helps them gain confidence in the role and, as a result, enables them to accept responsibility and accountability for their own development and performance as well as that of others.
- *On-the-job development*: On-the-job development can be a powerful experience in improving leadership performance. It can be conducted through a series of activities. For example, personal coaching, which allows for one-to-one exploration of what each person needs to do to improve their performance on the job. Team feedback can also be used as well as organisational feedback using organisational surveys. However, when surveys are used for on-the-job development, care needs to be taken to ensure the trust and credibility of the process. By doing this, more effective results will be possible and issues will be explored more fully.
- *Off-the-job development*: Off-the-job development usually includes structured leadership programmes, where individuals are able to practise and prepare for the leadership challenge by replicating the dynamics of strategic and leadership work in practice.

Summary points

- A manager holds a position in the organisation that comes with power and responsibility, but it does not mean that the position necessarily inspires people to 'follow'. Leaders need to generate 'followership'.
- Values are the beliefs that guide our behaviour. In an organisation where values are 'lived', they can be very influential in guiding staff behaviour without having to rely heavily on rules and regulations.

- To ensure values really are 'lived', they need to be turned into measurable practices. Measuring practices helps focus staff attention on what is important; it guides their behaviour and the future direction of the business.
- Leaders need to reflect the values of the organisation and be seen living them on a daily basis. Communication is a fundamental part of this and it is the leaders' responsibility to get this right.
- There need to be systems and processes in place to ensure that the values of the organisation are translated into strategies and practices which are, in turn, linked to managing staff behaviours.
- Leaders need to be able to create a vision or picture of where the company wants to go and then invest heavily in sharing that vision throughout the company. Visions should inspire and stimulate people into action.
- Leaders need to be developed across the organisation. Three key areas of leadership development are career development, on-the-job development and off-the-job development.

Further reading

Andrew Kakabadse and Nada Kakabadse (1999). *Essence of Leadership.* Thomson Business Press.
Alan Axelrod (2002) *Profiles in Leadership.* Prentice Hall Press.
Hugh Davidson (2002). *The Committed Enterprise: How to Make Vision and Values Work.* Butterworth Heinemann.

Best practice cases

Introduction

The two cases in this chapter have been selected to illustrate how leadership and values create a passion for customers. The first case focuses on Happy Computers (Overall and Small Business Winner 2003 and Business-to-Business Winner 2002). Happy Computers began life as a small, people-oriented training organisation running hands-on courses in all the popular PC applications. It continues to offer person-to-person training, but has also expanded into online delivery and is now expanding into non-IT topics. The company has grown from one person – founder Henry Stewart – to 43 staff over a period of 14 years. Happy has more than 4000 customers, over 90 per cent of whom are repeat customers. The company does not actively advertise its services, and has managed to grow on reputation alone. More than 15,000 people learn IT skills through Happy every year. Customers come from all sectors, though the company has a particularly strong presence among public sector and not-for-profit organisations.

There were many aspects of Happy's approach to service excellence that impressed the judges from creating a happy environment for their staff to work in, through to a happy relaxed environment for their customers to learn in. In fact it is fair to say that the 'Happy' philosophy permeates their whole business and every aspect of the Service Excellence Award.

The second case focuses on CragRats, a company founded by a pair of former schoolteachers, specialising in the use of theatre for communication and training for both the public and private sector. They were the Overall and Business-to-Business Winner of the 2001 Service Excellence Awards. The vision, which inspired the development of the Yorkshire-based company, was a series of strong value statements which would become enshrined in the business. This case study reveals how the founders were able to take these values and use them as the basis for building the foundations for a successful enterprise. In particular it considers how being a 'CragRat', coupled with a 'can do attitude', where the focus is on empowerment and allowing people to be themselves, is a formula which all the staff understand and respect.

Happy Computers ○ Happy People ○ Happy elearning

Happy Computers

Introduction

Happy Computers is a happy looking place, clearly designed by and for human beings. The company's offices on the edge of the City of London are painted in bright colours and fitted out with comfortable furniture. Its website has a cheerful, homemade look that belies the depth of information contained in it, and its links to the many glowing write-ups the company has received from an admiring media.

As a business that aims to train people in using computers, Happy lives at the toughest interface the IT world has to offer: the place where the power of technology meets the fear of its users. The mission of learning influences every aspect of Happy's operations, and it is in the mechanics and mysteries of learning where the company's success in the Service Excellence awards is rooted. A 1999 finalist and 2002 Winner in the Business-to-Business category, Happy Computers was the Small Business Winner in 2003 as well as the Overall Winner of the 2003 Awards.

Understanding how we learn

The key to Happy's success lies in its understanding of how adults learn. This understanding not only allows it to design and deliver effective training materials, but also to develop and sustain a culture that prizes service excellence above bottom-line performance. One way of describing Happy's insight into learning is as a tolerance for, and indeed encouragement of, mistakes. Stewart points out that children learn naturally by trying things out, making mistakes and developing alternatives. They do not associate mistakes with inadequacy, but discount them as steps along the path to eventual success. As we become more self-conscious about our performance, we grow to dread mistakes and see them as evidence of failure rather than as intermediary steps towards competence. And as adults, our abilities often come to define our status and security. Being unable to master a task instantaneously can make us feel angry, guilty or inferior. None of these states of mind is conducive to learning, with each pattern of thought tending to freeze our ability to accept new information and integrate it with our existing mental models. What adult learners need is a way of unfreezing or letting go, so that they can absorb new ways of thinking.

This is why relaxation is such an important element of Happy's approach. We tend to associate relaxing with shirking, in the belief that productive and responsible adults must be seen to be applying themselves to meaningful tasks at all times. However, the task of learning can only begin when the mind is receptive, and when the individual is confident of being able to make mistakes in a supportive environment. The bright colours and comfortable chairs at Happy Computers are part of the relaxation process. It is notable that enterprises typically apply this psychology in their reception areas but abandon it in the recesses of the office. Perhaps we should not be surprised if creativity and collaboration tend to stop at the doors of many organisations.

The importance of learning and feedback

Happy collects feedback from all its customers to determine how well it is meeting its objectives. The company regards any satisfaction score below 80 per cent as equivalent to a complaint, and reacts by contacting every member of the affected event. Customer feedback data is used to help design new courses and make changes to the service offerings, so that the learning circle is completed. Explicit complaints are investigated and dealt with in a 'no blame' style, with the team assuming by default that a service failure is a learning opportunity.

Happy Computers believes the expectations we create of others (and ourselves) of instant, perfect learning come about largely through frustration. It is not always easy to empathise with those who do not understand something we find easy, and it is often hard to remember that we ever faced such difficulties ourselves. But we tend to excuse such reactions in ourselves because we are not professional educators. We put the onus of learning on to the 'victim', and needlessly ramify the barriers to learning by maintaining a judgemental and guilt-laden attitude to their learning progress.

This could be a purely academic discussion with no business relevance: except for the fact that in today's highly competitive environment, the ability to put customers at the centre of the business's concerns relies on our people's ability to learn. They need to learn new skills and new ways of interacting with customers. They also need to learn about customer needs, and to be passionately interested in discovering and meeting those needs. Happy people need to find answers to challenges delivered by a customer-driven business environment, often crafting solutions that will never have been tried before. And in order to develop the business, organisations need to increase the number of mistakes they are prepared to make in pursuit of improved offerings and performance.

Trust is fundamental to success

Encouragement of mistakes goes against the grain of received management practice. The fundamental law of traditional management could be stated as the obligation to measure. In the classic management cycle, managers set (or negotiate) goals, design tasks, observe performance and then measure outcomes against goals. This approach naturally dictates layers of supervision, and plays to suspicions that people will fail or shirk in their duties rather than succeed as independent, trusted adults. Stewart marshals the experience of Happy Computers to refute the idea that control produces the best results: 'The key to our company is that people work best when they feel good about themselves. No one ever disagrees with that statement, but very few put it into practice.'

Trusting people can be the hardest step any organisation ever takes, yet the most productive. 'It's not rocket science, its basically about trust,' says Stewart of Happy's approach to business. 'Ask yourself: "What would my organisation be like if everybody was completely trusted?" And then think about what you need to do, in terms of training and support, to enable people to be worthy of that trust.'

The trust and creativity nurtured at the heart of Happy are evidenced in its ability to create new service offerings that rapidly capture lead positions in the learning provision market. For example, many training providers rushed into online learning as a potentially lucrative revenue stream. The cynical view was that existing training materials could be rapidly 'repurposed' for the web and new customers recruited at negligible cost. Training packages could be delivered automatically, grades awarded automatically and fees taken automatically. This is a neat line of business – in theory. But those who have tried this approach to learning have not scored significant successes. And such an approach would be anathema at Happy, given its commitment to people and its insights into the learning process.

Happy's move into online provision, therefore, incorporates the best of its people-centred approach with the efficiencies of electronic delivery. The online modules are combined with classroom sessions in a style called 'blended learning'. Extensive helpline support ensures that learners are never far from a friendly and knowledgeable coach. This approach retains the strengths of the online and human delivery channels, and crucially maintains full personal contact between the business and its customers. The rationale for the online offering is not solely as a means of expanding the company's delivery capacity, but recognition of customers' needs to study at times and places convenient to their work commitments and lifestyles. Happy's online product LearnFish is used in local and national government organisations as well as being the sole supplier to the National Health Service (NHS), where LearnFish is underpinning the delivery of European Computer Driving Licence (ECDL) certification to 450,000 NHS employees over a 3 year period.

Happy's staff!

A striking aspect of Happy Computers is the simplicity its principles bring to items of policy that cause problems in companies with less clarity of purpose. Happy believes in empowering people, and believes that learning enables people to achieve their potential. This belief is reflected in its own staff processes. So, for example, Happy's staff are encouraged to develop a work-life balance that suits their preferences, aspirations and feelings towards the community. Stewart spends one morning per week helping out at his children's school, while other team members work flexible hours or only during school-term time. Maternity and paternity leave are generous by UK standards, and every employee can spend one day per month on voluntary work.

Happy's administrative staff are known as 'smoothies', because they see their role as making the company run smoothly. This is a striking example of how a simple matter like role labelling can switch the focus of a team. While many companies regard adminis-trative roles as overhead, Happy sees them in their true light as busi-ness enablers. The job title's originality is another sign of Happy's interest in remaking the world of work to fit the people who do that work.

Having a strong mission and values naturally helps the company to take principled stands on issues rather than looking for ways in which to fudge them (see Table 5.1) Team members are encouraged to join a union, for example. All staff salaries are known rather than kept secret. Significantly, the company's smoothies wrote their own job descriptions after analysing their tasks and responsibilities and allocating them among themselves. By trusting its people, Happy simplifies a large proportion of its business processes. And by cele-brating the learning power of mistakes, it removes the need for a supervision culture or a system of sanctions.

The iconoclasm of Happy's people-centred principles is no more obvious than in its decision to give away training materials on its website. Most training organisations guard their intellectual prop-erty with fierce jealousy. Happy, on the other hand, believes that by giving away valuable content it encourages customers to approach the company while eloquently communicating its belief in personal empowerment. This is the kind of decision that organisations find hard to take, despite clear evidence from many successful online ventures that free distribution of content is a key element of creating customer loyalty and establishing relationships of trust.

Our Mission Statement

Our business is that of empowering people to reach their full potential in their work. Happy Computers' mission is to provide the highest quality training in the UK, creating standards which others follow.

To this end we will actively develop new training approaches, and other ways to help people learn, to enable all students to overcome easily any obstacles and be able to learn quickly and enjoyably.

Empower Our People

People are our greatest asset at Happy Computers. We have a responsibility for their training and for their personal growth while they are working with us. We will always look for ways to enable people to push back their personal limits and to reach their full potential.

If we treat our people excellently then we will receive excellent work in return.

Excellence in Everything We Do

We must strive to ensure that everything we do, we do excellently. We always look to provide the best possible service. This means that, however satisfied our customers, we must never be complacent. We must always ask how things could be better.

If we cannot provide a truly excellent service, then Happy Computers should not be providing that service at all.

The Customer

The customer is the whole reason for our existence and their needs must come before our convenience. We must listen carefully to all our customers and strive to find out (and to find new ways to find out) what they need and how we can help them.

If we cannot serve our customers better than our competitors (or at the same level for a lower price) then we should not be providing that particular service.

Innovation: Go Make Mistakes!

We must look for innovation in everything we do at Happy Computers – and particularly in the training process. Most people have lost much of their inherent capacity and eagerness to learn. A core element of Happy Computer's mission is to find new ways to enable people to regain that capacity and that eagerness.

Table 5.1   Mission and values

> Experimenting and innovation are crucial in this process. We must try out new
> ways of doing things and celebrate the mistakes we make along the way.
>
> ## Have Fun!
>
> We are in the business of empowering people and helping them to learn new skills.
> That is a challenging, but potentially very enjoyable experience. We must take delight
> in the process, including the obstacles and blockages which appear to get in the way.
> Relax and have fun.

Table 5.1   (*Continued*)

Small is beautiful

Happy Computers is a small business, and we might question its ability to scale its highly personal approach as the business grows. A concern for personal responsibility and a learning style is the hallmark of small, creative teams such as design agencies – the closest analogue of Happy in terms of corporate style and values. Can an organisation of a hundred or a thousand souls still roll with a culture that celebrates mistakes, or does it need tighter control – a greater reliance on rigid structures? Stewart believes that large monolithic organisations are unlikely to succeed in the long term, but that the style of Happy Computers can be applied at any sensible human scale. He finds inspiration in Ricardo Semler, the CEO or 'Counsellor' of Brazilian company Semco and author of *Maverick!: The Success Story Behind the World's Most Unusual Workplace* (Random House, 2001). Semco is a 'natural business' with a participatory management style. Full people empowerment includes the embracing of decisions a traditional CEO figure might disagree with. This kind of total involvement throughout the company retains the attributes of 'smallness' without imposing limits to growth. And just as Happy Computers can deliver learning to large numbers of people through deliberately small classes, so organisations can grow as collections of small groups.

A great place to work

The success of Happy Computers clearly owes as much to its values, work style and continuously renewed commitment to learning as its technical delivery skills. The contribution of its beliefs and culture is indeed so central to the company's capabilities that these aspects have become the foundation of a new offering. Happy is developing a 'soft skills' business known as Happy People. This service will help people to create organisations that are 'great places to work', in Stewart's phrase. This does not just mean creating organisations where people look forward to coming to work – although that is an important goal. There are sound commercial benefits on offer too. For example, the theme of relaxing to enable excellence finds further practical application in Stewart's observations of why many companies fail in their objectives: 'Most companies do know what their customers want, but they put processes in the way that stop it happening.'

Happy has always had the habit of sharing its approach, evangelising its values through organisations such as Inside UK Enterprise (IUKE), a service of Business Link. IUKE gives people the opportunity to visit selected companies or 'hosts' to learn how they manage their businesses. Each host runs a series of one-day sessions, which include presentations, discussions, site tours and a networking lunch. Happy's programme as a IUKE host includes a session on 'Great customer service': 'The first principle of great customer service is "treat your customers as you would want to be treated". The second principle is "don't treat your customer as you would not want to be treated".' It is a novel and challenging approach that stems characteristically from Happy's experiences of creating and delivering excellent customer service. The seemingly paradoxical principles lead directly to practical matters – in particular, the ability to recognise what differentiates great service from normal service. Happy's IUKE programme also includes a session on 'Creating a great place to work', which again focuses on practical actions and features a checklist of 22 steps organisations can take.

People are hired and promoted within Happy using straight-forward rules that ensure the best match between business requirements and team members. 'We believe if you're promoted to managing people it should be because you're good at managing people – which seems radical,' says Stewart. Managers are in fact termed 'co-ordinators', and their responsibility is to look after the development of the people in their care, rather than direct their activities. Co-ordinators are, therefore, selected on their coaching and nurturing skills rather than technical abilities.

The same kind of strong distinction is at work in the company's recruitment policy. Stewart is proud that Happy has never put a qualification requirement into a recruitment advertisement. 'If you really mean to hire people according to their attitude, then you should never put discriminatory things like "graduate" in your advertisements. That's shorthand for something else,' says Stewart.

Community work

It has long been fashionable for commercial organisations to make contributions to the community, though the taint of tokenism inevitably attaches to those companies who communicate their efforts too piously. The public often assumes that corporate charitable programmes are 'clean hands' operations, where the company writes a cheque to a worthy cause and then basks in a virtuous glow. This is generally an unfair assumption, since corporate donors are increasingly aware of the internal benefits of genuine contact with the causes they support as opposed to lip-service payments. Happy Computers' community involvement is typically hands-on. The company gives away around 25 per cent of its profits every year – an exceptional figure for any organisation, let alone one that does not have any obvious social or moral deficit to make up in the community which hosts it. Every member of staff can nominate a cause for a £75 donation, and the company stocks a timebank of 100 person-days per year for special projects. In 2002, two Happy team members spent a month teaching IT trainers in Uganda, and a similar project took place in Cambodia in 2003 and Nigeria at the beginning of 2004.

Stewart firmly believes that voluntary work brings many benefits to the company as well as to the clients served by each project. People who contribute to the voluntary work scheme derive great energy from it, and their experiences help to build rounded and committed individuals with a strong sense of self. There is a direct effect on skills as well, since team members who volunteer put themselves outside their usual settings. Of course, Happy would not be happy if it forced its people to do voluntary work. However, even among those who choose not to volunteer, there is a clear sense of pride at being in a company that whole-heartedly supports voluntary activities.

Conclusion

Happy's development work with IT trainers abroad echoes its core learning principles. These principles centre around involvement.

As the company's website puts it: 'Tell me and I forget. Show me and I remember. Involve me and I understand.' The aim of the learning approach is to get people acting for themselves. The sooner they can take responsibility for their own learning, the faster, deeper and more enjoyable their learning experience will be. It is worth noting that Happy's emphasis is very much on *learning* rather than *teaching*. Learning is something we do ourselves, with help and guidance, whereas teaching is something somebody else attempts to do to us. There is little doubt which emphasis produces the best results.

Happy also knows that learning is a journey of discovery. As a company, it is still learning how best to help its customers learn, and it confidently expects this to be a lifelong – and Happy – process. Meanwhile, the values of the company and the techniques it has developed to foster and communicate those values may help to create a new family of Happy companies. Just as the 'Easy' prefix has become a recognised brand in the consumer arena, indicating innovative approaches to providing traditionally upscale resources such as airline flights or cinema tickets, so 'Happy' may come to signify service excellence across a range of vertical markets. That would be one way for the Happy family to grow in line with its people-centred principles, while sharing its discoveries and methods with an ever-widening customer base. And maybe one day all organisations will be proud to stand for happiness as well as quality, value and service.

CragRats

Introduction

On 30 August 2001, the audience gathered at the Savoy for the annual ceremony of the Unisys/Management Today Service Excellence Awards and waited with baited breath to learn who would take the coveted prize for the year's Overall Winner. The name read out to enthusiastic applause was not one of the large national companies or household brands present that day; instead it was CragRats, a business founded 10 years earlier by a pair of former schoolteachers, and specialising in the use of theatre for communication and training. The Yorkshire-based company's submission had been in sharp contrast to many of the other leading contenders: where the others used systems, processes and reams of data to demonstrate the quality of their service, CragRats' strengths appeared to be founded in an altogether more natural and intuitive relationship with both customers and staff. But this is just one of the many ways in which CragRats has shirked convention. For this is an arts company that operates without subsidy and is run as a profitable commercial enterprise; it is a business set up without anything recognisable as a business plan, without investors or advisers; and CragRats has also invented its own market without recourse to market research, yet with a surefooted instinct that seems to defy many of the rules in the marketing textbooks. The pressing question for many who have first-hand experience of CragRats is whether the lessons it provides can be readily taken on board in larger organisations.

Starting out

CragRats was founded by Dave Bradley and Mark Greenop, who met as teachers at Hemsworth High School in West Yorkshire at the start of the 1980s. Both were highly successful in their school careers: the former was promoted to head of humanities and the latter became head of the creative faculty. Among their common interests they shared a love of climbing which provided an opportunity to take students on expeditions outside the school. It was during a climbing weekend in the Lake District in 1989, when Bradley and Greenop were holed up by rain on a boat on Derwent Water, that they started talking seriously about leaving education and starting a business for the first time. Something like 150 ideas were written down on a piece of paper, but the two reached no firm conclusion about the nature of the business they would start. What they did articulate, however, were some strong statements about the values that would be enshrined in the business.

These included:

- We wanted everyone who worked for us to grow and be as fully developed as they wanted to be.

- We wanted to have fun.
- We believed that the only way you can do anything valuable is where there is a sense of beauty, a sense of purpose. So that was the aesthetic: to make a difference.
- We wanted an entirely social collaborative team environment: all for one and one for all.

It remains a point of pride to CragRats that these values came before deciding what the company would actually do. The founders believed that if they had the right ethos, their staff would live it and would in turn communicate it to their customers, and that this was the essential foundation for a successful enterprise.

The direction of the business came about in part through accident. A former colleague had left teaching to work for one of the Government's Training and Enterprise Councils (TEC) in Barnsley and was looking for a way to inform impending school leavers about the Compact Initiative, a scheme in which year 10 students would make a series of commitments such as timekeeping, homework and good behaviour that would make them more attractive to employers. In return they would be guaranteed interviews when they left school. Greenop wrote a short play to sell the Compact Initiative to the students and their parents. There was no budget to hire actors: he and Bradley played all the parts. At the end of the performance, students could sign up, and the results were so successful in all the schools where CragRats put on its inaugural production that word quickly got around. The education and business partnership in Newcastle was looking for a way to communicate careers advice to schoolchildren. It signed CragRats for a tour of 70 schools. Initially, the business was run on a part-time basis, with both Bradley and Greenop continuing to teach. Actors were auditioned for the Tyneside tour, and by the end of 1991, the founders had given up their day jobs and set themselves up with a fax machine in some converted pig-sties at Greenop's farmhouse. They also took on their first full-time employee.

Bradley learned the rudiments of running a business by attending more than 30 business development courses sponsored by the Dti. One that left a deep impression was on 'how to become a millionaire'. 'The second night we were told a golden rule: find a niche market and dominate it. Our niche market soon became the TECs.' CragRats stumbled into this market without any market research. The original intention had been to work for the corporate sector, but when the TECs and other quasi-public sector clients came along, they were warmly embraced. As to using theatre as a communications tool, the nearest precedent was to be found in educational theatre companies, heavily dependent upon subsidies, which had mainly disappeared when their grants were cut by the Conservative government. The idea of a performing theatre company operating on purely commercial lines was a novel one.

Video Arts, the video training company set up by John Cleese, had demonstrated that there was a market for alternatives to flipcharts and PowerPoint presentations in communication and training. But Greenop and Bradley believed that as a two-dimensional medium, video's power to communicate was limited. By performing to their audiences in person, they believed they could truly engage their hearts and minds. Neither of them ever doubted that it would work, they say. This confidence was born in part from their experience of using drama in school and elsewhere. 'I'd been doing similar stuff during my sabbatical with the New York Police Department, on how they treated people in the Bronx, and I knew it worked,' says Greenop. But their climbing and outdoor activities had also invested the pair with a powerful sense of self-belief in their ability to make things work.

Growing the business

From modest beginnings – turnover was £7000 in year one – CragRats grew rapidly and had sales of £100,000 after 4 years. There was little need for advertising or the other marketing skills that Bradley had learned on evening courses, the work 'just came in' with corporate clients soon joining the TECs and other public sector bodies. In 1996, CragRats moved into a new headquarters, a former mill in the Yorkshire town of Holmfirth. The five-storey building was purchased for just £70,000, and extensive work was carried out on renovation and conversion. For the first time CragRats had to borrow money. The business had been entirely self-funding until this point, and for the first three years the founders did not even take out a salary.

In 1998, a theatre and cafe-bar were opened on the ground floor. The theatre acts as a touring venue for small-scale drama, music, dance and comedy, including an extremely popular Christmas pantomime; it can also be hired out. The cafe-bar attracts the local community and serves as an in-house meeting place. It also led CragRats to diversify in 2000 into corporate catering. More recently, CragRats bought a nearby country house to provide better accommodation for actors. From its initial concept of providing bespoke theatre-based presentation, CragRats has developed a series of brands – Action Training, Conferencing, Event Management, Digital Media production, Production, Careers Education, Entertainment, ReAct (issues for young people), Theatre and Corporate Catering. The company employed 44 people full-time and 10 part-time in December 2001, with turnover expected to reach £3.6 million during the financial year. It has also become a significant employer of actors – who are self-employed – with up to 150 on tour for CragRats at any one time.

Service with a spine

From the outset, there has been a philosophy at CragRats that if its own people understand the values that the company stands for, they will live these values and will in turn communicate them to customers. In practice, there is no specific training on customer service. The company depends heavily upon 'recruiting for attitude' which means that it is vital to select those who demonstrate the right level of commitment in the first instance. At the heart of the CragRats philosophy is a belief that real customer care comes from allowing people to be themselves, rather than presenting them with scripts or even a prescribed tone for communication. This is summed up as: 'We simply treat people the way we'd like to be treated on the phone.'

Staff work in a closely-knit open plan environment and are expected to provide feedback to each other if one of them is doing something wrong. In gauging customer satisfaction, there is less emphasis on measurement – albeit more than 250,000 customer evaluations are collected each year – than on obtaining qualitative feedback. Every client is telephoned after the event in order to get feedback. CragRats' people are encouraged to be honest and direct with their customers. As Greenop puts it: 'You have to be direct with your customers, sometimes tell them: that's crap. Sometimes you have to be brutal with them. It's about honesty. You have to say "trust me" when clients are nervous.' Equally, though, one of the company's philosophies is 'to encourage self-esteem of those who work for and with CragRats'. Forthright interaction, in other words, must be constructive in its nature.

The notion that some customers are more equal than others gains little support at CragRats. The ethos is to always do the best, whoever the customer is. An example is given of a relatively junior training manager at BT who recommended CragRats to his superiors, landing them with their biggest single piece of business, the BT FutureTalk project. This is summed up as: 'the person in front of you is always the most important'. CragRats also has a strategic view that it is important to give extra value – to deliver more than the customer has signed up for. In part this stems from a desire to challenge clients, to push them further than they are comfortable with. But it also has a sound commercial basis, since it makes it harder for anybody to compete with CragRats.

To be a CragRat

At CragRats there is a well-established notion that somebody either is, or is not, 'a CragRat'. This seems to be largely intuitive, although there are some tangible characteristics that are sought. 'They have got to have respect, belief and passion. They've got to want to progress,' says Greenop. In other words, CragRats are expected to be self-reliant, to engage fully with their work, and to have a level of ambition – even if that is not necessarily along conventional career lines. An example of someone who is not a CragRat is an actor who refuses to join with other members of the team in unloading the van and other assorted tasks on the road. In fact, flexibility and absence of demarcation are hallmarks of employment at the company. Employees sign a contract which, along with outlining their basic duties, adds '… and anything else'. On one occasion, the entire office was closed so that everybody could help out at an event being staged for Cadbury's; on another, staff and managers dropped their work to stuff envelopes for an urgent mailshot to schools.

The founders are nevertheless adamant that there is not a single template for a CragRat. Some employees are noticeably extrovert, others much less so. The philosophy is that they should be allowed to be themselves – so long as they adhere to the company's values. The aim is to pick the right people at the recruitment stage, but all employees face a three-month trial period, and managers do occasionally get it wrong. However, turnover of staff is reported as 'extremely low' less than one per cent annually.

CragRats places a strong emphasis on empowerment for its regular employees too, which extends not just to making decisions, but to how they organise their work. For example, there are virtually no regular scheduled meetings; most tend to 'just happen', often in the kitchen. If two people have a problem with each other, they are expected to sort it out between themselves, rather than approach a manager. The approach is not so much laissez faire as one of self-reliance, and stems from a belief that in order to learn, people have to make their own mistakes – although not to the cost of a customer. And it is not inconsistent with discipline. A small number of employees have been sacked: a chef who failed to turn up for an assignment; an actor who smoked cannabis during a tour; and an actor who could not learn his lines. Any misconduct that risks damaging the CragRats brand is treated very seriously, particularly because of the link with schools. Support is provided in a number of ways. A buddy system has been introduced, so that every member of staff has an opposite number who can do their job if they are away or sick. It is recognised that some mentoring – or intensive supervision – is needed, especially where somebody has taken on a new job where a new skill set is required. People tend to learn on the job rather than being sent on external courses, but CragRats encourages those taking external qualifications, and does hold occasional 'company days' where everybody works on issues together. Staff congregate in the cafe-bar after work, but there is little in the way of regimented socialising.

It is not the money

The strategy regarding reward is to focus on providing an environment in which people are fulfilled, rather than offering financial incentives. Pay and conditions for actors are above the levels required by the actors' union, Equity, and include free accommodation – in a recently acquired country house – as well as a commitment to pay wages at the end of each week (in contrast to other employers in a sector renowned for late payment). Paradoxically, many of the salaried employees earn less than they could elsewhere; quite a few have left much higher paying jobs to work for CragRats. This appears to vindicate the assertion that money is not the main motivator for employees. They are not offered other financial incentives such as bonuses, profit share or share options, in the belief that this would prove 'divisive' and would distract from the team ethos. This state of affairs is probably accepted by employees because the two owners of CragRats lead by example, reinvesting profits in the company and leading a relatively unostentatious lifestyle.

Reward also comes in other forms at CragRats: through being engaged in work, and caring about it, rather than just doing a job; through working in an environment with a palpable buzz about it; and through being able to realise potential as an individual. One of the outstanding characteristics of CragRats is the way that people have been allowed to move into jobs that they wanted to do, when other companies would have ruled them out because of lack of experience or the 'wrong' background. For instance, one employee, Rob Machon, came in to do some plastering work, and persuaded Bradley and Greenop to let him run the cafe-bar at its inception, through dint of his enthusiasm. He is now general manager. Another employee who left school at 15 to run a milk round is now in charge of the company's accounts. Everybody is asked on a regular basis if they are happy with what they are doing, or whether they want to move to a different job.

CragRats also has an unconventional take on recognition. There is no 'employee of the month' scheme, no material awards of cash or vouchers as many companies practise. Instead, recognition consists of people being simply thanked for outstanding efforts.

Directors and managers attempt to speak to each member of staff at length every week, so that they know when recognition is deserved and praise can be given. Nobody has to wait for their annual appraisal. The founders of CragRats were in fact resistant to the idea of having a formal appraisal, and only agreed to do so when staff asked for it. Now, employees are set individual targets at their appraisal, but these may be more personal and less conventional than in many other companies: for example to keep your hair cut tidily or to be aware of the fact that others find you intimidating.

Just do it

Since the company's inception, there has been only minimal reliance upon formal business plans, and although each brand team does have an ongoing plan, with budgets and targets, the accent is on flexibility and it is subject to constant revision. The directors of the business take the view that a rigid business plan serves little purpose as it is almost certain to prove wrong and is, therefore, a hostage to fortune. By the same token, new ventures have been approached in an ad hoc fashion, rather than through in-depth market research and feasibility studies. CragRats has been able to do this because of its financial solvency; with no need to borrow money, it has been able to proceed without the need to make a carefully argued business plan. New ventures seem to have relied upon a combination of factors: intuition, closeness to customers and expediency. The cafe-bar was conceived because there was a vacant space on the ground floor of the building. The idea to move into corporate catering came from the cafe-bar's manager, who suggested: 'We've got great food, let's sell it to some of these companies'. But it was also underpinned by the knowledge that some clients were looking for food to go with their events.

There is a discernible tension between Greenop's desire to act with spontaneity – summed up by the motto 'just do it' – and Bradley's instinct to take a more controlled approach. The two seem to be finely balanced, with CragRats managing to remain creative and dynamic, at the same time as being able to pay out up to £45,000 a week in wages, without encountering cash flow problems.

The future

CragRats clearly faces a number of key issues in the next few years. At its current level of growth, it will outgrow its existing premises fairly quickly, and have to decide whether to remain on a single site, or whether to move to a number of sites. This will also have a knock-on effect on the way the business is currently run. As the company grows larger, it is hard to see how the short lines of communication and the personal interaction between directors and individual members of staff will be sustainable.

The two founders have inevitably begun to take more of a back seat with respect to the day-to-day running of CragRats, and are focusing much more on innovation. Their vision for the future includes a 'CragRats Resort' including theatre, conference, restaurant, hotel and other facilities all under a single roof, and encapsulating the CragRats culture. In this vision, which they hope to realise within the next five years, CragRats would be seen as a way of finding meaning, and obtaining complete enrichment. The values first hatched on a boat in the Lake District back in 1989 have already achieved a great deal; just how much further they can go remains to be seen.

Chapter 6

Organisational agility

Introduction

Change is one of the great certainties of business life, and how well an organisation responds is a measure of its agility. Organisations today find themselves increasingly challenged by having to manage unpredictable and continually changing customer opportunities. Forecasts become unworkable and success is dependent on an ability to respond rapidly and flexibly to customer requirements, to change gear and immerse the organisation in these new opportunities on a constant basis.

The notion of organisational agility has its origins in flexible manufacturing systems, where it was believed that automation alone would confer this capability. Over time, a wider business application has emerged, led by developments in supply-chain management. An acknowledged expert in this field, Professor Martin Christopher from Cranfield School of Management, defines organisational agility as a 'business-wide capability that embraces organisational structures, information systems, logistics processes and, in particular, mindsets'. The agile organisation creates competitive advantage for itself by being able to adapt its people and processes to the continually changing needs of the marketplace, increasingly with the support of technical innovation. The challenge for organisations is to fuse together people and process approaches to achieve cost-effective value delivery. Competitive advantage today lies in recruiting and motivating the right people, giving them the most appropriate tools and training, while at the same time constantly improving business process. When either element, people or process, fails to embrace change, the organisation becomes less nimble and therefore less able to compete.

Organisational agility forms the final vector of the Service Excellence model. It is the last stepping-stone to achieving customer focus that brings with it profit and growth. In the Service Excellence model agility is implemented through information and action:

$$agility = information + action$$

Information and the management of information have risen up the organisational agenda and now comprise a major business discipline, known as knowledge management. The aim of knowledge management is to build a collective and dynamic corporate memory. It has been driven by advances in IT and growth in the use of the Internet, which allow information to be exchanged across the world, 24 hours a day, seven days a week, all at the touch of a button. Failure to adapt knowledge management practices to the continually changing environment leads to what has been described as 'corporate amnesia', a phenomenon that prevents organisations learning from their own experiences.

Therefore, in order to support organisational agility, an organisation needs to master the flows of information throughout its value chain. As Lew Platt, former CEO of Hewlett-Packard, has often been quoted as saying, 'If Hewlett-Packard knew what Hewlett-Packard knows, we'd be three times more profitable'.

Agility then becomes viable depending on how strongly the organisational culture encourages and embraces change. Best practice organisations encourage constructive criticism and see that their staff receive the appropriate tools and training to cope with change. In an agile organisation, people respond positively and confidently to change.

This chapter

This chapter examines the role of organisational agility in creating customer service excellence by looking at how well organisations anticipate and respond to the changing world. This is based around the five key questions in this vector of the self-assessment questionnaire:

- Constructive criticism is an essential element of our culture.
- The organisation provides methods, tools and training to enable change.

- We have tools and techniques that facilitate the capture and sharing of knowledge and expertise.
- The organisation monitors and shares information about the changing socio-economic environment.
- Our people respond positively to change.

The role played by each of these elements is explored in more detail and then demonstrated through case studies of two previous Awards winners: The Veterans Agency and BAA Fit Out team.

Constructive criticism is an essential element of our culture

Change management is most ably delivered by organisations that encourage their employees to challenge the decisions and plans of their managers without having to fear any form of retribution. As Michael Dell, founder and namesake of the world's leading computer services provider, says, 'One of the challenges of a company that is succeeding is that you run the risk of complacency'. He encourages his team to explore incremental improvements and to experiment with ideas that add value, primarily in terms of efficiency. This means fostering an organisational climate where employees feel comfortable challenging the status quo. This was demonstrated by a recent Service Excellence Awards entrant who claimed 'our team meetings are a two-way process where constructive criticism is expected'.

Successful, agile organisations evolve their own unique approaches to engendering this sort of climate. It can often depend on the level of cross-functional collaboration between marketing, operations and human resource management departments. The focus of this combined resource is ensuring that there is alignment between the value proposition offered to customers and that offered to employees. For example, previous Awards winners Countrywide Porter Novelli, a successful business-to-business PR consultancy, operates what it calls the 4Is culture:

- Imagination – making our work memorable.
- Irreverence – challenging the status quo.
- Improvement – a little better every time.
- Initiative – making the first move.

This articulation of principles does not simply take the form of a bright logo to be used in communications, but provides a framework for managing delivery of the value proposition both internally and externally. It represents a distinct advantage that Countrywide Porter Novelli believes it offers clients, and guides the recruitment, training and promotion of staff internally. Unusually, the director of personnel and development and the marketing director sit down together to discuss joint implementation of the internal and external marketing strategy on a regular basis.

This way of working represents a set of values that support the vision of customer service excellence. As discussed in detail in Chapter 5, values are the beliefs that guide behaviour within the organisation and they need to be embedded throughout: in organisational structure as well as human resource practices such as recruitment, training, appraisal and reward schemes. It is also important that they are embedded in internal debate (as with the system of team meetings mentioned earlier) and in succession planning (ensuring that any new leader understands the ethos and past history of the organisation).

The organisation provides methods, tools and training to enable change

In order to capitalise on the advantages of creating a culture where constructive criticism is an essential element, organisations need to ensure that they invest in equipping employees to manage change. This is because although positive attitudes to 'irreverence at work' and a climate of encouragement go a long way towards enabling change management, employees also need to be able to call on the most appropriate tools and training. What gets offered will vary according to the experience and history of the individual organisation. However, best practice organisations are distinguished in that they employ a portfolio of approaches as a means to an end, as a way of working towards improved levels of customer service excellence.

Some organisations work to identify a common approach to change and then ensure this is diffused throughout. For example, this may include common formats to running meetings and post-project appraisals. It is also routine for organisations to adopt common tools across functions. Formal change management training programmes are widely deployed and organisations distinguish themselves by deciding whether to run these in-house or use a third party to do this for them. Some organisations then make the most of joining forums for sharing experiences and best practice in what are essentially benchmarking operations. The Service Excellence Awards provides one such example of the way in which these schemes and programmes can offer a useful source of more objective feedback on an organisation's efforts to manage change. Two useful metrics in all of this are first, to track over time the percentage of people in the organisation that have undertaken formal training of one sort or another in managing change and secondly, to audit how many days of change management training were provided across the organisation in any one year.

Schemes and methodologies such as the CharterMark quality model, ISO 9000 and Investors in People are used by best practice organisations to help them equip people to manage change, and identify and implement improvements in customer service excellence. Organisations that embrace the learning to be gained from adopting a portfolio of methodologies, tools and training find that they start to move beyond formal training to managing change as a way of doing business. This works to produce an ever greater level of agility.

We have tools and techniques that facilitate the capture and sharing of knowledge and expertise

Knowledge management is now recognised as a strategically important business process that can make or break an organisation's reputation for customer service excellence. It has been transformed by developments in IT.

The first step in creating a knowledge management system is to establish a process for capturing knowledge about the organisation, its customers and the business environment. There are two main types of knowledge to be managed: these are known as explicit knowledge and tacit knowledge. Explicit knowledge is the more tangible of the two. It represents the type of knowledge that can be captured in written or process form and is easily reused. The 'what' dimension of corporate 'know-how' is made up largely of explicit knowledge. Tacit knowledge, on the other hand, refers to the implicit and often ambiguous knowledge that is acquired mainly through personal experience. It is usually context-specific and provides the 'how' dimension of corporate 'know-how'. Tacit knowledge is difficult to formalise and hard to capture. As people are generally better at talking about experiences than writing them down, new techniques to capture tacit knowledge are emerging, many of them based on the art of storytelling.

Knowledge itself, of course, has no intrinsic value as its value comes from being used, and, unlike any other business resource, knowledge grows with use. Extracting and exploiting the value of knowledge to deliver customer service excellence is a core competence of Awards winners. Previous winners, PetCareCo Limited (formerly known as Triple 'A'), provide a useful example of the way in which the integration of technology and knowledge management into service delivery is transforming many organisations. The PetCareCo case study features in Chapter 4, Engaging People, and describes how the staff at this one-stop pet resort and care centre based in Washington, Tyne and Wear, provide superlative standards of pet care while their owners are on holiday. The business is staffed by a team of dedicated animal lovers who are supported in their work by a sophisticated, but easily manageable, range of technology. For example, handheld devices are used to carry daily pet care schedules and a back office system records data on every pet, enabling the company to instantly recognise and recall any previous 'guest' history, and use it to make the pet feel welcome and at home. The aim is to ensure that every animal gets the right service, at the right time, in the right place.

The organisation monitors and shares information about the changing socio-economic environment

Every MBA programme around the world will cover – at some point – at least one session on the importance of formally scanning the marketplace and understanding the forces that may impact on its future stability. Students learn to categorise these forces with acronyms such as 'PEST analysis': the political, economic, social and technological trends that may offer new opportunities and threats. Others extend this acronym to 'PESTEL' by adding on environmental and legislative trends. Regardless of which is favoured, it is important that an organisation makes provision to understand the key trends that may impact on the environment in which it operates. These trends need to be monitored on a continual basis, and not merely looked at as part of a once-a-year planning exercise. This has implications for the scanning and planning activities within the organisation. The aim today is create on ongoing process that better reflects the dynamic complexity of the marketplace rather than relying on conventional approaches that set down the three- to five-year ambitions of the organisation in a static plan.

What matters most is the interpretation of these trends and again, classic business school learning can be drawn on here. It was business guru Michael Porter who identified five forces that determine the intrinsic profit attractiveness of a market or market segment: industry competitors, potential entrants, substitutes, buyers and suppliers. Each of these may represent a threat to the organisation: the threat of intense segment rivalry (or an over competitive situation in a certain segment); the threat of new entrants; the threat of substitute products; the threat of buyers' growing power; and the threat of suppliers' growing power. This model provides a comprehensive way of assessing how changes in the external environment may impact the organisation and is used to great effect by both commercial and not-for-profit organisations.

The mark of an agile organisation is one that not only monitors information on the changing environment, but shares it through organisation-wide systems that are linked into decision-making processes. This contrasts with less customer responsive organisations where some of this information is gathered but not widely shared.

Our people respond positively to change

Organisations that can demonstrate that their people embrace change as natural and essential are those who can rightfully claim that 'it is part of our culture to treat change as the norm'. Awards winners continually question what they do and the way they do it. They compare their performance with others and consult with customers and staff. Many have done away with traditional hierarchies and replaced them with largely self-managed teams supported by a small management team.

Making the shift from an organisation where change is viewed with concern to one where employees respond positively and confidently to change as a way of life, requires building an organisation-wide capability that is embedded in organisational structure, processes and people management. In adapting both people and processes to the continually evolving opportunities in the marketplace, the agile organisation creates competitive advantage for itself.

This approach is exemplified by 3M, a company that continuously and consistently demonstrates success in the marketplace. At 3M (UK) employees are given the freedom to take risks and try out new ideas, and this has led to a steady stream of new products. John Mueller, former Chairman and CEO of 3M (UK), is quoted as saying, 'We want to institutionalise a bit of rebellion in our labs. It has been said that the competition never knows what we are going to come up with next. The fact is, neither do we'.

However, marketing creativity at 3M is carefully balanced with financial control. Performance is assessed by evaluating the results of its innovations: 30 per cent of annual company sales must be generated from products less than four years old, and ten per cent from products less than one year old. This distinction is refined in two further categories, with new-to-the-world developments being looked upon as 'the ideal' versus the substitution of new products for old. This represents an analysis of performance at a base level that can then be extracted down to smaller segments of customers, and can also be translated internally into departmental, team and individual targets. 3M realises the importance of enabling its people to see their own picture in its vision for the organisation.

Summary points

- The agile organisation creates competitive advantage for itself by being able to adapt its people and processes to the continually changing needs of the marketplace.
- Constructive criticism in the workplace is an essential element in overturning corporate complacency.
- Organisations need to invest in tools and training to enable their people to manage change effectively.
- Knowledge management aims to build a collective and dynamic corporate memory, made up of explicit and tacit knowledge.
- Understanding of the political, economic, social and technological forces at play in the market needs to be linked to decision-making processes.

- Positive and confident attitudes to change need to be embedded in organisational structure, processes and people management.

Further reading

Martin Christopher and Helen Peck (2003). *Marketing Logistics*. Butterworth-Heinemann.
Alan Harrison and Remko van Hoek (2002). *Logistics Management and Strategy*. FT Prentice-Hall.
Probst, G., Raub, S. and Romhardt, K. (1999). *Managing Knowledge: Building Blocks for Success*. Wiley.

Best practice cases

Introduction

A business that is focused on delivering truly responsive service excellence is a business that can 'turn on a sixpence' and make the most of the opportunities and challenges it faces. The two case studies presented here illustrate this well. The Veterans Agency (Public Services winner in 2001) is responsible for assessing and paying pensions to disabled servicemen and women and their spouses in the UK. This case reveals how it coped when faced with the kind of administrative task that many other organisations would find daunting. As Lorraine Smith, Business Excellence Manager at the Agency, comments, this is an organisation that has learned how to 'absorb new challenges'.

The second case focuses on BAA Fit Out, the project delivery team that provides construction and logistics services to BAA airports at Heathrow, Gatwick, Stansted and Southampton. The Fit Out team were overall winners in the Manufacturing/Engineering category of the 2001 Service Excellence Awards. They impressed the judges with their consistently agile and innovative response to projects that often involve them in having to carry out much of their work in short time windows at night when airports are not working. All of this is done with the interests of their customer's customers – the passengers – at heart.

VeteransAgency
An Executive Agency of the Ministry of Defence

Veterans Agency

Introduction

During 2001 and 2002 the War Pensions Agency, a part of the Department of Social Security, changed its name and its organisational home. The organisation became the Veterans Agency, and moved to the Ministry of Defence (MoD). The repositioning of the Agency, in both its widened customer scope and improved reporting lines, is a testament to the Agency's success in making efficient payments to ex-service people with care and compassion. The continuing success story of the Veterans Agency is rooted in excellent customer service, and in particular its extraordinary organisational agility.

The British government introduced the War Pensions Scheme in 1917, following the huge number of casualties in the Great War. After the Second World War the scheme was expanded to include ex-members of the Polish Forces who served under British command, merchant seamen and civilians injured due to enemy action. War pensions work was relocated from London to Blackpool, where the Agency still operates today. More recent conflicts such as those in the Falklands, the Gulf, Bosnia, Kosovo and Afghanistan also come under the scheme.

The foundations of the scheme have changed little since it was established, although a war pension can be paid for any service-related disablement and is not confined to wartime activity. The Agency serves some 271,000 customers, over 26,000 of whom live outside the UK in more than 100 countries. Some £1200 million is channelled through the scheme each year.

There are around 920 staff members at the Agency, ensuring that claims are met promptly and accurately. Communications with customers are handled with sensitivity and respect. There is a clear sense of admiration for customers throughout the Agency, and a strong commitment to their interests. There is no doubt that Veterans Agency staff see themselves as both servants of, and advocates for, the people they call 'our brilliant customers'.

With legislation in its area of activity rarely changing, and its main traditional customer base shrinking naturally over time, the Agency might seem an unusual focus for organisational agility. Its challenges are not the more obvious ones of competition and innovation that characterise most commercial sectors. The Agency's customer base is smaller than that of many public agencies, and more easily defined. Yet the Agency's unique role and relationship to its public service environment have created acute challenges to its organisational agility, and provoked responses that have wide-ranging lessons.

A test of agility

The best example of the Agency's agility, and the experience that has done most to earn its respect among peers, was its handling of the payments ordered for Second World War prisoners of war (POW) held in Japanese camps. The government gave the Agency this task in November 2000, with tight deadlines for the disbursement of the £10,000 payments.

This was a large and complex task, involving many thousands of claims and checks on top of the Agency's usual workload. The Agency welcomed the responsibility, and set about delivering the goal, with every member of staff involved. A rapid pilot exercise was held, with the close involvement of campaigners for the payment. The Agency had always maintained a special section for dealing with claims from the Far East theatre, so there was already a good partnership relationship between the organisation and the target customer group. In fact, the strength of these customer relationships contributed to the allocation of the task to the Agency in the first place, since there were other government units who might also have received the challenge.

The Agency quickly realised that a dedicated group would need to be formed to deliver the project. But the creation of such a group would mean major disruption throughout the organisation. Agency skills are not easily replaced by outside help, so managers were unable to employ temporary workers on a one-for-one basis to cover for displaced staff. A complex process of shuffling and sharing resulted in temporary staff being brought in to support the more general clerical functions, freeing up Agency staff to help each other fill the gaps created by the formation of the project group.

None of the reallocation of responsibilities could have been achieved without the enthusiastic support of all those involved, and their determination to make the project a success. It is a clear case of a common cause galvanising a highly customer-oriented team. Everyone accepted that they would face some pain, and all areas of the agency gave up staff to the project, right down to operating hotlines outside work hours.

Just dealing with this sudden tide of work might seem challenge enough. However, the Agency also recognised that the project provided a clear opportunity for the organisation to grow its competences. The project demanded that the organisation extend its traditional services to include identifying potential recipients of the payment; normally, customers are fed automatically to the Agency from the MoD. In the case of the Japanese POW payments, Agency staff had to research wartime records and deal sensitively with people who had experienced extreme deprivation, and had waited a long time for recognition and compensation. The project became a personal cause for many who worked in the customer-facing roles, with customers writing to the agency to express their surprise and satisfaction at the efforts made on their behalf. The Agency processed more than 25,000 claims and made 20,000 payments during the intense 6-month period. Veterans Agency staff took the project to heart, as well as using their heads.

The move to the MoD

Extraordinary demands often bring out the best in people. Are more normal times at the Veterans Agency as impressive? The Agency's relocation to the MoD suggests that they are. The move to the MoD was actively embraced as an opportunity to enhance existing service delivery, reach a wider customer base and develop the capabilities of staff still further.

Staff had never been entirely happy with the historical accident that made them part of the Department of Social Security, latterly the Department for Work and Pensions. They never felt that the Agency's customers should be managed alongside other groups of claimants, in recognition of the service those customers have provided to the community, and the sacrifices they have made on our behalf. In practical terms, the practices and systems of the DSS did not always match the Agency's requirements. A new payments system imposed on the Agency by its parent in the 1990s disrupted its work and, more importantly, alienated its customers. Agency customers were used to receiving personal letters from the organisation – letters which had been hand-typed as late as the early 1990s.

The new, bulk-printed letters with their simplified language and checkboxes were not appropriate for the Agency's older customers.

Insufficient training within the Agency and a reliance on external consultants did not help matters. Yet Lorraine Smith, Business Excellence Manager at the Veterans Agency, says that the experience 'made us stronger'. The turmoil made Agency staff realise the depth and strength of their customer orientation, and the extent to which their attitudes differed from those of other organisations. The experience also taught them that they knew their own requirements better than any outside expert. Their confidence in their own knowledge was based soundly on their strong customer relationships, and their culture of acting promptly, flexibly and sensitively to customer needs. That these lessons were learned and that they further strengthened the organisation is evident in the way the Japanese POW project was given to the Agency. There was no suggestion or expectation that the Agency would not achieve the goal itself, or that it would look to a third party for help.

Keys to success

One key to its success is the Agency's careful monitoring of key performance indicators (KPIs). Performance measures are highly visible within the organisation, and published in regularly updated form to the public via the Agency's web site. The performance measures are sophisticated enough to demonstrate that even where the delivery of a customer service goes wrong, customers still rate the service highly. This discovery is yet to be made by many commercial organisations.

Another key to its organisational agility is the Agency's approach to staff involvement in change. Staff at all levels can challenge, contribute to and constructively criticise decisions. Internal focus groups are often used to tackle new or revised processes.

This commitment to inclusive and visible management is reflected in the openness of the Agency's main operational tools. The Programme Review Board (PRB) meets monthly to explore the Agency's workload in its entirety. All new items and any issues involving current work are considered, analysed and challenged according to clear criteria. These criteria include optimum business delivery, full support of the Agency's agreed strategies, priorities and values, as well as affordability and manageability. Changes to the work programme are managed through a dedicated programme office and an explicit change control process. The Agency's agenda, and its progress, are therefore visible at all times to the whole team.

Management team Phone Days and Staff Forums also provide staff with an opportunity to air their views or ask questions about Agency business. In a recent staff survey, 87 per cent of all staff felt their manager always or usually listens to their ideas.

A model of customer orientation

Surveys continue to show that the majority of Agency people regard change positively, appreciating the essential role of change in delivering continuous improvement in the business. Substantial changes in the Agency's structure and operational processes have rolled out alongside continued performance improvement against targets in each year. The average time taken to process a claim has declined from 146 working days in 1994/1995 to 73 working days in 2001/2002. This is well within the target of 90 working days. The Agency's target for accuracy in processing claims is 94 per cent; it achieved 96 per cent in 2001/2002. Delivering new and improved services while improving both customer and staff perceptions at the same time is no easy feat, but the Agency has achieved both through a combination of individual dedication and organisational strength.

The Agency ensures that it is never a 'faceless bureaucracy', no matter the length or complexity of a case, by assigning named staff at all points in the process. This process starts when a new claim is received, with an executive caseworker from the assigned team telephoning the customer to introduce themselves. Customers know that their interests are being pursued by real, accountable individuals.

The Agency runs a programme of Lunchtime Presentations where speakers from other areas of the MoD, ex-service organisations and other bodies help staff to gain insight into aspects of service life or disabled living. Topics in the programme have included 'Life as a Civilian Internee' and 'A Guide Dog Owner's Story'. The lunchtime events are always over-subscribed. Other awareness initiatives include a development programme called Understanding Disablement which provides staff members with short-term placement in services for the disabled, and allows them to participate in a Ski Bob event for amputees held annually in Austria. These education and awareness initiatives create very close identification between staff and their customers. Few organisations commit to this level of immersion in customer concerns – but the benefits in terms of enhanced customer relationships are reflected throughout the Agency's operations.

The Agency's clarity of vision, based on the primacy of its customer relationships, is a guarantor of its enduring organisational agility. Agency people admire their customers. They take the time to learn about the types of disability that their customers have, as well as the types of experiences they have had. This strong identification with their customers as real and worthy individuals makes organisational agility second nature for Agency staff.

Within its new home at the MoD, the Agency now has the opportunity to show leadership as a key player in the comprehensive government 'Strategy for Veterans'. This new strategy includes not only those who have served in the UK Armed Forces, but also their widow(er)s and dependants. This makes a large and diverse community of some 13 million people in the UK alone. The Strategy addresses communications between veterans, the government, the voluntary sector and the general public. The Veterans Agency has a key role to play in the Strategy as it develops, not just as a customer-facing contributor in its own right, but also as a complementary team working with other agencies in the government and voluntary sectors.

Lorraine Smith recognises that reconciling the fluidity of change with the need for stability is at the paradoxical crux of organisational agility. Her answer to the paradox is rooted in the talents and attitudes of the people who make up the organisation:

> I can only be complimentary about the workforce here. Everyone here feels our customer is worthwhile, and our service is worthwhile. So you've got to carry on, *and* you've got to meet the extraordinary demands too. If we stuck to business-as-usual we'd be quickly out of business, so we've got to move on. We have to absorb the new challenges.

The Veterans Agency's performance against its 2001–2002 targets agreed with the MoD

Target	Achievement
Putting service first Secretary of State Target: To deliver a quality service to war pensioners and war widows by achieving the standards published in the War Pensions Agency's Service First Charter	
Management targets • To issue decisions on claims to war pensions within an average of 90 working days	✓ 73 working days

(Continued)

Target	Achievement
• To issue decisions on war widow(er)s claims within an average of 36 working days	✓ 25 working days
• To visit all recently-bereaved war widow(er)s within 15 working days of a request being received	99.86 per cent of visits within 15 working days
• To achieve a claims accuracy rate of at least 94 per cent	✓ 96.17 per cent of claims were assessed as accurate

Working in partnership

Secretary of State Target: To reduce the average time it takes an appeal to pass through the war pensions appeal process. By 31 March 2002 the average time should reduce by 10 per cent from 2000–2001 baseline levels	Time reduced by 42 per cent

Management targets

• To clear appeals to war pensions within an average of 195 working days at Stage 1 of the process	✓ 135 working days
• To clear appeals to war pensions within an average of 15 working days at Stage 3 of the process	✓ 11 working days

Modernisation and managing change

Secretary of State Target: To implement the recommendations of the War Pensions Agency's Decision Making and Assessment Review to the standards and timetable agreed with the Department of Social Security	✓ achieved

Valuing our people

Secretary of State Target: To lead and manage people effectively through specified measures and contribute to the reduction in public sector sickness absences by 22 per cent from 1998 Public Service Agreement baseline levels by 31 December 2001	✗ not achieved, see Note 1

Efficiency

Secretary of State Target: To generate efficiencies during 2001–2002 to absorb the effect of pay and price pressures; and to improve efficiencies so that the Agency operates within its running cost allocation	✓ achieved

Note: 1. The transfer of personnel records from the Department for Work and Pensions to MoD has disrupted the Agency's recording of sickness absence data. Consequently, the Agency was unable to measure sickness levels across 2001. Data the Agency had available, however, indicated it was unlikely to achieve its 2001–2002 target.
Source: Report by the Comptroller and Auditor General HC 522 Session 2002–2003: 28 March 2003 Improving Service Delivery: The Veterans Agency; http://www.nao.gov.uk/publications/nao_reports/02-03/0203522.pdf

Performance – VA Published Service Charter Standards: 2002/2003

Service Charter Standard	Target	Achieved year to date (April 2002– March 2003)
Decisions on claims to war pensions should be issued within an average of 82 working days	82	62.66
Decisions on war widow(er)s claims should be issued within an average of 34 working days	34	24.49
All written enquiries and complaints should be acknowledged within 5 working days of receipt	5	97.75 per cent
All written enquiries and complaints should be responded to within 10 working days of receipt	10	98.15 per cent
All Chief Executive correspondence should be responded to within 15 working days of receipt	15	97.64 per cent
Calls to the VA Helpline should be answered within an average of 20 seconds	20	18.3 seconds
All visitors should be attended to within 10 minutes of their appointment/arrival, whichever is the later	10	99.92 per cent
All recently-bereaved war widow(er)s should be visited within 15 working days of a request being received	15	99.93 per cent
A claims accuracy rate of at least 95 per cent should be achieved	95	98.00 per cent
Appeals to war pension should be cleared within an average of 175 working days at Stage 1 of the process	175	136.00
Appeals to war pension should be cleared within an average of 100 working days at Stage 2 of the process by March	100	136.22
Appeals to war pension should be cleared within an average of 15 working days at Stage 3 of the process	15	10.60

Source: http://www.veteransagency.mod.uk/aboutus/per02-03.htm

BAA Fit Out

Introduction

Organisational agility is not just a nice-to-have at BAA's Fit Out team: it is the team's reason for existing. Agility is a key ingredient of its industry environment, but for Fit Out agility is the determinant of all its activity. The team is responsible for rebuilding functional areas of airports with minimal disruption – in a business where seconds are measured in millions of pounds and the most rigorous standards of safety permeate every action. It is a mission that has Fit Out pulling a multi-storey building out of its pocket and erecting it in a few short hours in the middle of the night. Their mission is causing the team to reinvent the construction industry from the inside out.

Fit Out is a project delivery team that provides construction and logistics services to Heathrow, Gatwick, Stansted and Southampton airports. The team operates as an individual business entity with an independent operating budget. It is a virtual organisation that embraces suppliers and specialists outside the BAA family.

A core team of 60 staff members leads 11 partner companies, acting as a design and build organisation. Employees from the partner companies are seconded into the team's virtual company environment.

Fit Out serves several different customers, including airlines, retailers and passenger facilities management. The team also works for BAA's property department and its World Duty Free business. This is a very diverse customer base, with each customer having a distinct specialism. Their different business objectives, combined with the highly dynamic nature of their activities, make them demanding customers. Add in 24-hour operations in a high-tech, security-conscious environment and you already have a set of requirements and constraints that would stress any business, even before taking into account the specific details of any one project. The only way the team can carry out successful constructions in the airport environment is to adapt its business to complement that of its customers. The Fit Out team's aim is to become the 'invisible builder'.

A modular approach to design and construction

The Fit Out team characterises itself as a delivery team working within a logistically challenging environment, with a large capital spend. These conditions impel it to lead its industry in the invention of new approaches, and the adoption of available best practice from other areas. The team's Clive Coleman cheerfully admits that they will take successful ideas from anywhere they can find them. The team uses Activity Based Planning, for example, a tool borrowed from the American manufacturing community, and runs a 'One In A

Million' safety initiative modelled on a programme used in the oil processing industry.

Although Fit Out is keen to adopt and adapt whatever tools it can to further its mission, it is also committed to innovating where necessary. The main focus of the team's innovation is its modular approach to the design, build and installation of airport components. This is the key to its 'invisible mission' strategy.

The team's unique answer to its unique pressures is to create a manufacturing approach to construction. Construction is traditionally carried out onsite, with materials, labour and project management being brought together in a circumscribed, controlled area. Construction sites typically put physical areas out of normal action for long stretches of time. They also allow different trades to contribute their skills and solve problems as they arise. Traditional construction, although controlled by blueprints and manifests, incorporates a large measure of give-and-take, sometimes dictated by the peculiarities of the site, but often arising from the space and time given to the project.

The manufacturing approach, on the other hand, demands standardisation, and is less tolerant of deviation in process or materials. The principles of manufacturing stretch back to the standardisation of parts for the guns of the American Civil War and the rationalisation of processes in Ford's early factories. Industrial production brings us goods of high quality and reliability, at low prices, and with speed. But it does not usually bring us buildings.

Fit Out's solutions form a kit, or a palette, of modules that can be mixed and matched to create final building components. By combining elements in different ways, the team can build airport components that look completely different to each other while actually being formed of identical components. A departure lounge at Gatwick's North Terminal, for example, will appear different to one at Heathrow's Terminal 3, even though its elements come from the same kit of parts.

Fit Out likens its kit of parts to domestic kitchens. Kitchens appear to offer a wealth of choice to the consumer but are in fact based on a limited set of standard components. The dimensions of carcasses and worktops, for example, are standardised throughout the industry. Choice is created by the wide variety of finishes, closures and accessories that can be applied to the basic kit. These secondary components provide a huge number of permutations. In a similar way, Fit Out produces a range of 110 standard products, each of which can be customised in a number of ways to suit specific uses.

Benefits of a modular approach

The first place in the value chain where this approach saves time and money is the design phase. Architects and designers normally start projects with blank sheets of paper – but starting from scratch is expensive. In Fit Out's world of rapid construction, many fundamental design decisions are removed from the process, leading to a much quicker start. At the same time, the solution kit approach provides greater predictability to the project, right from day one. The use of standard parts implies known costs and lead times, so the project plan is generated from the initial kit selection.

By inventing and implementing this approach, Fit Out has put itself firmly on the cutting edge of its industry. New methods are not always welcomed in industries with entrenched habits and trusted, traditional ways of meeting customers' requirements. The virtual nature of Fit Out has helped to carry suppliers along with the vision. By being part of the team, rather than a partner relying on instructions, the first tier of suppliers have embraced the approach and quickly come to see how it enhances their own businesses.

The airline business is in itself a very agile industry. Airline schedules change every 6 months, so the industry works to a 6-month planning horizon. Airports themselves are, as any traveller will testify, works-in-progress; they are never 'finished'. The snapshot state of an airport at any one time is a measure of its evolution towards new goals. And yet airports have to be fully usable at all times. Therefore each site is in a constant state of change, yet required to give seamless service.

The dictates of the airline business create very short decision-making timelines. The Fit Out team responds to this reality by offering solutions where precise definitions can be left open as late as possible. The team's modular approach to construction effectively allows it to compress the construction schedule.

Move to offsite working

The Fit Out team is steadily shifting construction activities offsite. The team has invested in the manufacturing approach because it is the logical answer to their dilemma: how to build quickly, flexibly and reliably, and with an eye to cost control. Its strategy has led to improved quality and reduced costs, while extending the real choices of its customers and upgrading the skills of its component members.

The team sees itself as a supplier of products to its customers, rather than services. This is one sign that the manufacturing approach runs through its whole operating ethos. It defines its products as 'interior space transformation', which map to specific items including shop units, departures and arrivals lounges, concourses, piers and link bridges. All the team's products have to work alongside products from other delivery teams, which supply shell and core buildings, baggage handling systems and infrastructure.

The move to offsite working might seem like a neat, if novel, solution to the difficulties of working in the airport environment. In fact, building onsite is becoming increasingly untenable as the airline business's own agility continues to load new demands on the environment. Night-time slots are shrinking as airports become busier. Night working is also expensive, with a typical 4-hour slot billed as a 12-hour shift at time-and-a-half rates. At the same time, the number of functions targeting the available slots for maintenance and enhancement activities is growing. Fit Out's window of opportunity is therefore constantly shrinking. With an environment that is in a state of constant turmoil, Fit Out is forced to evolve new capabilities to survive.

Managing within the constraints of the business

The team also faces other practical constraints that force it to preserve and improve its agility. One of these factors is the shortage of labour in the south east of England, where BAA's primary operations are located. The region is enjoying a construction boom. BAA is contributing to the load on the industry through its high-profile Terminal 5 project at Heathrow. But T5 is just one of the projects that will generate a doubling in the company's construction efforts over the next few years.

As if the squeeze on construction slots and labour were not enough, Fit Out must accommodate a stringent security system. Airports have always been highly secure sites, but the terrorist attacks of 11 September 2001 have tightened controls still further. Every worker requiring access to an airport must have security clearance. The rigour of the required checks can mean a delay of up to three months for the issuing of a pass – a delay which would undermine Fit Out's compressed timelines.

Fit Out's answer to these constraints is to pre-empt them. It accommodates itself to the ever-shrinking window by improving the range of its pre-built solutions. It solves the labour problem by creating its components using manufacturing skills and techniques, and locating these operations in low-cost areas wherever possible. The team honours the airports' security requirements by reducing the number of people it requires to have onsite, by pre-clearing the staff that it does need onsite, and by using a pool of people with security 'passports' wherever possible. These strategies put the aim of complementing its customers' business into inventive action.

A radical approach to innovation

The organisation's latest innovation is a facility based in Crawley for manufacturing very large structures such as piers. The team has been building smaller components using offsite techniques for some time, but the new facility represents a major step up in scale. Here, entire buildings are put together using the latest manufacturing techniques from heavy industry. Inspired by the flowline technology used by the Airbus consortium to build aircraft wings, Fit Out have created a manufacturing environment where the construction project moves between work teams on rails. The final product is large, but not so large that it cannot be transported by road. The facility's current site at Crawley balances the costs of construction and haulage, though subsequent 'building factories' may be located elsewhere. Some £20 million to £26 million worth of construction flows through the Crawley factory every year. This is a substantial figure in its own right, but it is a fraction of the alternative cost that would be accrued in building in the traditional way – if the traditional way remained a viable option.

Fit Out has also taken the imaginative step of bringing large-module construction techniques to non-intrusive areas of an airport site, and then using the taxi-ways to manoeuvre the completed structure to its permanent position. Five-storey buildings have been assembled and installed in this way, though the team prefer to work on slightly smaller scales with this strategy. A typical example is a two-level bridge intended for Terminal 3 at Heathrow. The bridge, designed to span the gap between the terminal and a pier, was around 75 metres long, some three storeys high, and weighed 1000 tonnes. It was built near Terminal 4, then moved during the night and hoisted into position. Though the bridge appeared overnight, the project as a whole took a year.

Another spectacular project involved building a bridge to cross a taxi-way catering for wide-bodied aircraft. This was the first such

bridge of its kind anywhere in the world, and to build it in the traditional way would have cost £11 million, including the cost of divert-
ing the taxi-way around the construction site. Fit Out constructed
the bridge at the edge of the site and then moved it into position
during a single week.

Such feats are spectacular, but rare. Fit Out's continuous impact
on its customers comes from its day-to-day agility in meeting the
less glamorous, but equally vital, requirements of its demanding
environment. For example, improvements to security at airports
are driving the increased separation of arriving and departing
passengers. Some sites already comply with this requirement, but
BAA is making a £250 million investment to reconfigure four termi-
nals to bring them into line. Fit Out has developed a common
solution set for this challenge, and is also taking between 40 per cent
and 50 per cent of the working hours required for each terminal
offsite.

Improving agility at Fit Out

Adding a new element to an airport is not quite as easy as Fit Out's
modular approach perhaps makes it sound. This is because no
airport was built from the ground up using a modular approach.
Although Fit Out can offer excellent agility and value for money
through its standard products, interfacing those products with their
real-world destination requires some level of customisation. The team
therefore needs to apply a measure of flexibility in the installation
phase, which again requires an agile response. Any failure to make the
components work on the ground would negate the elegance of
the modular approach, destroying the compressed timelines by which
the team lives.

The team recognises that there is great to scope to improve their
performance further. Fit Out's targets include the goal to deliver
65 per cent of the assets it builds as standard products by 2005. The figure currently stands at around 25 per cent. The team believes it can
meet this target by continuing to apply the modular principles it has
already implemented. The further target of reducing the hours spent
by the team onsite by 65 per cent is more stretching. Many infrastructure tasks, such as paving runways, are inherently difficult to
accomplish elsewhere than their required positions. Pursuing new
technologies and management strategies is a continued focus for the

team as they work to win this goal. This fits well with the ethos at BAA, which Coleman describes as 'doing well, doing better: keep raising the "doing well" bar.'

Fit Out is also a good example of a virtual organisation succeeding in practice. The team's members form an extended organisation that overlaps BAA's traditional boundaries. The structure promotes a partnership approach to projects, and to long-term investment in facilities, skills and techniques. Construction projects can often become adversarial, being designed around contracts. Fit Out's projects are collaborative ventures where suppliers are encouraged to make their own decisions within a holistic approach. Breeding flexibility into the team's approach is vital for ensuring that customers retain the right to change their requirements right up until the last possible moment.

Further management challenges

The heightened sense of speed within Fit Out brings two further challenges to management. One is that the continuous nature of change within the delivery environment makes it difficult to appreciate progress at the micro-level. As Clive Coleman says, 'You never actually see the minute hand move. You have to measure over time to see improvement.' This is a very different situation to what we find in transaction-based businesses, where improvements can rapidly be measured in terms of volume.

The second management challenge is related to KPIs. Within the Fit Out team itself, a core set of KPIs remain relatively stable, with some evolution demanded by the need to keep raising the bar. However, the team's KPI are often impacted by changes within the wider company. The composition of the KPI dashboard changes frequently, meaning that KPI collection and interpretation rarely become a matter of routine.

The team is not daunted by this variability in metrics. Indeed, Fit Out's appetite for benchmarking shows that the team relishes finding new ways of measuring its progress. It has performed benchmarking exercises within BAA, and is increasingly benchmarking against external organisations. An ever-increasing commercial focus at BAA, tied to the innovative nature of Fit Out's solutions, is driving the team to compare its activities with other types of construction assets, and with other industries.

Looking ahead

When it won its Service Excellence Award in 2001, Fit Out had reported impressive results that it would be hard for any organisation to beat – including itself. The on-time, on-budget project completion rate was 94 per cent. Timeframes and costs had tumbled, while the team's safety record had continued to score well above industry norms. Its goals for the future show that Fit Out still sees great room for growth, and is not tempted to be complacent.

Fit Out is proving how radical solutions to problems set in complex environments can be both developed and implemented in a repeatable fashion. When agility is non-negotiable, innovation and standardisation can produce quality, value for money and speed. It is to the team's further credit that they have managed this transformation across a disparate group of partners in a focused, virtual organisation. Fit Out's pursuit of organisational agility is reinventing the way organisations are built, as well as airports.

Chapter 7

Service excellence best practice

Introduction

Service excellence is about taking an integrated approach to business that puts the customer at the centre of everything it does. Making it happen is – as this book demonstrates – about managing a number of different processes within the organisation. However, the task is not simply to manage them on a stand-alone basis but instead to embrace the fact that they are interrelated and will impact on each other. Each of them plays a unique role in enabling the organisation to deliver customer service excellence and together they can elevate an organisation above its peers in the marketplace. Every year the judges in the Awards scheme look to find best practice examples across a range of categories – retail and consumer, financial services, manufacturing/engineering, business-to-business and public services. And every year there is stiff competition for the coveted awards. The Overall Winner's Award is given to the one organisation that impresses the entire team of judges with its service excellence practice. In 2002, it was the Nationwide Building Society that stood out from the platform of sector winners and it is this organisation that provides the final case study.

However, before introducing Nationwide's story and revealing why it won, the first part of this chapter reflects on the general lessons to be learned from the Awards scheme. Here the Unisys/ Management Today Service Excellence Award is reprised and briefly explored through its constituent elements, customer intelligence, operational effectiveness, engaging people, leadership and values and organisational agility.

Customer intelligence – summary

Service excellence is underscored by a compelling business philosophy that promotes the establishment of long term, mutually trusting and profitable relationships with customers. The first step to building this philosophy within an organisation is to have in place processes to generate customer intelligence. The aim of these activities is to develop a sense of customer intimacy, and Chapter 2 explored the ways in which organisations build their knowledge and understanding of their customers' needs and expectations, and how customers perceive the performance of the organisation. These were illustrated through the cases of Woburn Safari Park and Rackspace Managed Hosting.

While no one research tool or technique provides absolute customer intelligence – organisations need to blend a portfolio of methods in an ongoing process – this information provides an essential foundation on which the organisation can build its offer to customers, and affords an insight into the changes in products and services that customers may be looking for. It helps provide insight into customer motivations to buy, and can supply knowledge and understanding of the competitive frame within which the organisation operates. This information can be leveraged through the process of segmentation, which works to portion the market and identify the most profitable sectors (however they may be defined) on which to concentrate the organisation's resources. This process is essential as it enables the organisation to be confident about the market in which it operates, providing the answer to the simple but strategic question, 'What business are we in?'

Adopting this outside-in approach to strategy development enables the organisation to define the value customers are seeking from the *customer's* perspective. Organisations need to understand how customer value is made up: the elements that maintain value, the value enhancers and the value destroyers. This chapter also examined the notion that innovation in service excellence is about creating new solutions (in *how* the organisation does something as much as *what* it does) that are acknowledged by customers as offering real value.

Customer intelligence best practice organisations, like Woburn Safari Park and Rackspace, are able to respond positively to the following statements:

- We encourage and act on feedback from customers.
- We understand the drivers of customer satisfaction.

- We are recognised as innovators in our market.
- We build long-term profitable relationships in our chosen markets.
- We monitor and track customer retention and repurchase intention.

Operational effectiveness – summary

Chapter 3 established that customers continue to turn to particular companies because they are easy to do business with. For organisations, achieving this means creating their value offering around an understanding of exactly what it is customers desire. Best practice organisations express this in terms of the four Cs (customer needs and wants, cost, convenience and communication), rather than the four Ps (product, price, place and promotion). This understanding then forms the focus of the organisation's activities. In many respects, it means turning the supply chain on its head and thinking about taking the customer as the point of departure for the organisation, and not its final destination. Making this an operational reality is then dependent on the effectiveness of service delivery processes and programmes.

For many organisations, the aim of operational effectiveness is to deliver the 'perfect customer experience' on every occasion. This is not, however, a single event but is best conceptualised as an ongoing process. And in order to ensure that service delivery processes and procedures are optimised, best practice organisations use one or more sets of tools and techniques to promote continuous improvement. These may include benchmarking, the International Standards Institute's ISO 9000 series or Six Sigma. This latter approach, based on established techniques developed in manufacturing, has been popularised through the impact it has had on the Motorola and GE businesses. Essentially, Six Sigma is a statistically based, organisation – wide approach to quality improvement that aims for a maximum number of error-free transactions, generally expressed as so many per million occurrences.

Awards winners take this data driven-approach very seriously and also ensure that they can track the cost of servicing a single transaction; and many also track the costs of non-conformance. These are the costs incurred when the organisation fails to do things right first time. These may include costs of rework, administering complaints or discounts or refunds to customers.

Operational effectiveness has become a lot more complex in light of the proliferation of media and channels. And for organisations with a multimedia/multi-channel strategy, their goal is to ensure that the customer has a perfect experience across all the media and channels they offer. Each time the customer comes into contact with the organisation, they should feel like they are talking to the same person. Too many organisations forget this when it comes to integrating the web into the service offering – for them it offers an opportunity to cut costs rather than enhancing the customer's experience.

Finally, organisations need to manage their customer complaints – excellent complaint handling consists of three key operational activities: dealing with the customer, solving the problem for the customer, and dealing with the problem within the organisation. A philosophy of proactive service recovery can work to improve service excellence.

TNT and the Dental Practice Board illustrated best practice in operational effectiveness and are typical of Awards winners who can state unequivocally that:

- Customers consider us easy to do business with.
- We enhance business performance through continuous improvement.
- We can deal equally effectively with customers over multiple channels.
- We deal with service failures effectively.
- We use the web to enhance the customer's experience.

Engaging people – summary

This chapter looked at the role of employees in creating and delivering service excellence. For many organisations, the quality and history of the relationships that staff have with customers remains the most unique aspect of their business. Competitors can copy many other elements but are less likely to succeed here. It is, therefore, not surprising that engaging people in the organisation has become a boardroom agenda item.

This represents a shift away from the time when the business environment was dominated by manufacturing and employees were regarded as a production cost that needed to be controlled and reduced. Today, service-based organisations recognise that their employees are, in fact, a capital asset whose intrinsic value can be grown, and their approach to employee management reflects this.

It is accepted by best practice organisations that employee behaviour, whether it directly or indirectly impacts the customer, plays a critical role in determining the level of service excellence that is experienced by customers. This will, in turn, influence customers' level of satisfaction with the company and affect their willingness to either remain with or defect from the organisation. The extent to which quality employees can be attracted, kept and motivated is therefore directly linked with the organisation's capacity to offer quality services to their customers.

Engaging people starts with having a vision within the organisation that forms the focal point of a climate and culture that inspires the hearts and minds of all employees. In best practice organisations this vision is communicated through all stages of the recruitment, training and retention process. Many service excellence companies believe in the careful selection of staff and search for individuals whose values and motivation match the organisation's service ethic. They adopt the philosophy that employee suitability should not just be based on technical skills, which can be taught later, but on characteristics which show a positive service attitude. And once they become an employee, the organisation then works to ensure that individuals have the right skills and knowledge to perform their work well. Best practice organisations distinguish themselves in this respect by going beyond the provision of training, which takes an organisation only so far, and creating a learning environment for their staff. This is characterised by a repeated pattern of study and practice, where learning effectiveness is measured by testing the results of what employees do, rather than measuring training effectiveness through testing people.

In high performing organisations, employee satisfaction is taken as seriously as customer satisfaction and reward, recognition and empowerment feature as a part of the organisational culture. These are organisations like case study exemplars PetCareCo and John Pring & Son who are able to respond positively to the following statements:

- Our people have the right skills and knowledge to perform their work well.
- We regularly monitor employee satisfaction and act on the findings.
- We recognise the performance and behaviour of outstanding individuals and teams.
- We empower our people to deliver service excellence.
- When recruiting and developing people we focus on attitude first.

Leadership and values – summary

Chapter 5 positioned leadership and values as the cornerstone of the Service Excellence Awards as they are intrinsically linked with the direction and culture of the organisation. How an organisation is led and managed determines its position within the marketplace. Leaders are not, however, the same as good managers; managers may have a certain amount of power and responsibility but this does not mean that they inspire people to follow. This is the hallmark of leaders – they generate what has been called 'followship'.

'Followship' is defined as a 'capability to lead [that] must be coupled with the practical skills that leaders need to have to manage their day-to-day affairs'. Among the skills that leaders need to demonstrate is an ability to command and focus resources on the attainment of a particular vision. This is a statement that provides the answer to the question 'where are we going?' It needs to become a shared idea of why the organisation exists and what it wants to achieve.

It is also important that leaders reflect the values of the organisation, in other words the preferred behaviours that will guide the organisation on its journey. Allied to this is a need for a high degree of people skills, to be able to manage the complex human interactions that take place within organisations, as well as good conceptual skills and sound judgement.

The values of an organisation are sometimes referred to as the 'ethos' of a business, or the 'principles', 'guidelines' or 'rules', and while the vision may change, values should stand the test of time. Their purpose is to guide behaviour within the organisation and where they are 'lived' by employees, organisations find that they come to rely less on formal rules and regulations. Staff understand what is expected from them, they know how to behave and how to respond to new or unforeseen circumstances.

However, there is often a gap between the values espoused by an organisation and the values customers and employees experience in everyday life. These are organisations where what gets preached does not get practised. Service excellence organisations work to narrow and, where possible eliminate, this gap. Senior managers who actively champion customers can play a crucial role in achieving this. Another fundamental differentiator of service excellence organisations is that their values feature the customer in at least one of their value statements. In too many organisations, references to the customer are missing.

The roles of leadership and values were explored in some depth in this chapter through the cases of Happy Computers and CragRats. These top scoring finalists were able to show that:

- Our values are widely understood and practised.
- Leadership reflects the organisation's values.
- Our processes of management enact our values.
- Senior managers actively champion customers.
- We invest in developing leadership across the organisation.

Organisational agility – summary

Chapter 6 looked at managing service excellence in light of the challenge of unpredictable and continually changing customer opportunities. How well an organisation does this is a measure of its agility. This concept first originated in flexible manufacturing systems but over time a wider business application has emerged, led by developments in supply-chain management. Defined as a 'business-wide capability that embraces organisational structures, information systems, logistics processes and, in particular, mindsets', the agile organisation creates competitive advantage for itself by being able to adapt its people and processes to the continually changing needs of the marketplace, increasingly with the support of technical innovation.

In the service excellence model, agility is implemented through information and action:

$$agility = information + action$$

The aim of knowledge management processes is to build a collective and dynamic corporate memory, made up of explicit and tacit knowledge. Failure to adapt knowledge management practices to the continually changing environment, where the Internet and e-commerce are changing the nature of the exchange with customers, leads to what has been described as 'corporate amnesia', a phenomenon that prevents organisations learning from their own experiences.

Therefore, in order to support organisational agility, an organisation needs to master the flows of information throughout its value chain. Agility then becomes viable depending on how strongly the organisational culture encourages and embraces change. Best practice organisations encourage constructive criticism and see that their staff receive the appropriate tools and training to cope with change. In an agile organisation, positive and confident attitudes to change are embedded in organisational structure, processes and people management.

The cases of the Veterans Agency (formerly known as the War Pensions Agency) and BAA Fit Out Team provide relevant illustrations of organisations that have an enviable agile approach to their very different businesses. In each case, however, they are able to demonstrate that:

- Constructive criticism is an essential element of our culture.
- The organisation provides methods, tools and training to enable change.
- We have tools and techniques that facilitate the capture and sharing of knowledge and expertise.
- The organisation monitors and shares information about the changing socio-economic environment.
- Our people respond positively to change.

Service excellence: best practice cases

The case study chosen for this chapter is Nationwide. They were winners of the Financial Services and Overall Service Excellence Award in 2002 and were selected to illustrate an integrative approach to service excellence. Financial services organisations are not often held up to be paragons of virtue when it comes to customer service excellence. However, Nationwide was found by the judges not only to be leading the pack in its field but also to have such superior practices that it merited the coveted title of Overall Winner. Nationwide had won the Financial Services Award two years previously in 2000 and in the intervening period had honed its processes to enable its 13,000 staff to deliver exemplary service to its 10.5 million customers, who are also its members owing to Nationwide's mutual status.

Being a building society with mutlal status means that the value created in the business is returned annually to members, rather than to outside shareholders. This makes members at once both customers and owners of the business, creating a more complex relationship to be managed. Nationwide, as the case shows, believes this to be the strength and that it provides a real focus for customer service.

The judges were impressed with many aspects of Nationwide's approach to service excellence but especially their understanding and management of the link between employee satisfaction and organisational performance. This is explored in some detail in the case. However, it was not simply the internal focus of the organisation that struck the judges but also the way in which Nationwide works to collect customer intelligence. In many respects their initiatives are leading edge, and demonstrate a real commitment to defining and creating the service excellence customers seek. As Philip Williamson, CEO, says, 'We're passionate about this. If we do these things, the members will love us.'

Nationwide

Introduction

Nationwide won the Service Excellence Award for the Financial Services sector in 2000, and returned in 2002 to win it again – and scoop the Overall Winner Award into the bargain. Nationwide has strengths across all the dimensions assessed by the Awards process, so it is a truly holistic example of best practice in service excellence. The organisation's mission to serve customers continues well beyond its achievements in the awards, which is a sign that the attitudes and habits of service excellence can become part and parcel of the day-to-day activities of even the largest enterprise.

Nationwide's success begins in its recognition of the powerful principles established by its 1996 decision to remain a mutual building society owned by its members while competitors were transforming themselves into publicly listed companies. Mutuality provides a very clear and consistent connection between the actions taken by the organisation and the people who benefit as a result. Identifying Nationwide's stakeholders is not hard: they are the more than 10 million savers and borrowers who use the society's financial products and services. Improving the business therefore has an unambiguous goal: returning value to the members. In this case study we look at how the society is doing just that, as reflected in the facets of the Awards assessment structure.

Customer intelligence

To start, we can see that *customer intelligence* is far advanced at Nation-wide. Nationwide believes wholeheartedly in collecting, analysing and acting on customer and employee feedback. On the customer side, Nationwide distributes 28,000 surveys every month. These are triggered by service interactions. With more than 1.3 million transactions taking place across more than 600 branches and electronic channels, this is an effective sample rate. The response rate is nearly 28 per cent, a significantly higher rate than most such surveys, and all the more impressive for being achieved without the use of any incentives.

Tim Hughes, Nationwide's Head of External Affairs, stresses that understanding customers requires organisations to think holistically about customer situations. He says that many organisations tend to research customer satisfaction with existing purchases without checking to see if their circumstances have changed. 'It's like asking someone if he's still pleased with his Ferrari when he's suddenly acquired two children. He may well still like his Ferrari, but he might now be looking at buying a people carrier,' says Hughes. Consequently Nationwide's customer intelligence activities look to relate satisfaction with repurchase decisions.

The society's Usability Centre is a world-class example of customer involvement in the design and development of new products and services. The centre is purpose-built to simulate the different interaction environments Nationwide offers: branch, call centre, home and even in-car. Products tested in the centre can be scored for usefulness, effectiveness, efficiency, satisfaction, respect, presentation and learnability. The target is an 80 per cent or better rating on each dimension. Results are presented in the form of spider graphs, which quickly highlight any aspects of the product that need rethinking. Presentation of data in the spider graph format is a common practice elsewhere in the business, helping to communicate complex information quickly and clearly.

Nationwide's approach to customer segmentation appears unusual at first, since the society does not work to a sophisticated segmentation scheme that seeks to stereotype customers and drive sales to them. Although the organisation researches carefully to discover and meet customer needs, it does not use its research to engineer exclusivity into its offerings. So, for example, Nationwide has three types of credit card product designed to appeal to three types of customer, but does not assume that any one particular customer is only suitable for one product. Customer circumstances change and even the best customer information can lag behind. Hughes says: 'We would not seek to embarrass a customer by offering something for which he wasn't qualified. But our aspiration is to have customers with products across the range.' Nationwide's mass-market focus, coupled with its mutual status, means that for this organisation differentiations in service are based on customer need rather than customer value.

The organisation's recently introduced ICRM system allows customer-facing staff to advise customers about the product range, based on their transactional history. However, this is very much an advisory system and a guide to customer interaction rather than a sales system. In fact, Nationwide does not link personal performance targets directly to sales, believing that such a connection creates the wrong behaviours.

Operational effectiveness

On the dimension of *operational effectiveness*, Nationwide is particularly notable for its Brainwaves employee suggestion scheme. This is a Society-wide scheme delivered via the Intranet. Brainwaves offers rewards for service improvement ideas which are implemented in the field. In one ten-month period, the society's staff generated 3591 suggestions resulting in 520 implementations and cash awards of £24,024.

Nationwide uses feedback from members in a practical manner as well. In the year of the society's second award, the organisation applied more than 200 improvements stemming directly from members' experiences of service failures. The society publishes a leaflet telling the members of these actions, so that the feedback loop is completed.

As a two-time winner, Nationwide is a fine example of how entrants to the awards can use their experience of preparing an entry and receiving the assessment to improve their business. Following the 2000 award, Nationwide launched a series of projects under the banner of the First Choice Programme. The projects included Customer Satisfaction Surveys, Internal Service Measurement, Dispute Resolution and Employee Empowerment.

Focusing on the Dispute Resolution project, Nationwide introduced a new Internal Complaints procedure to encourage all customer-facing staff to take ownership of complaints and agree a resolution at the earliest possible opportunity. All complaints and feedback are recorded in a Complaint and Feedback Log hosted on the society's Intranet. The log gives staff shared visibility of complaints and current progress towards their resolution. It also helps them actively manage the resolution of complaints, providing guidance on best practice in complaint-handling, key employee contact lists, letter templates and management information reports. The introduction of the new complaints procedure and log system in December 2001 helped to improve performance in service recovery, enabling effective complaint handling at the first point of contact. Assured continuity of attention and the inbuilt progression features of the procedure and its supporting system mean that dispute resolution is an intuitive, speedy and well-resourced feature of the society's customer service rather than the 'Cinderella' area found in some organisations.

Nationwide's proactivity in Operational Effectiveness is also reflected in its Service Improvement Plan, which covers all customer-facing teams. Customer feedback and benchmarking information on the society's products and services is collated and used as the basis for the plan. The plan is used as a mechanism to convert the feedback into actionable service improvement recommendations for the customer-facing areas. Monthly update meetings with each of the teams are held, ensuring the plan is in constant focus and allowing new recommendations to be added into the plan.

The final measure of Nationwide's success in Operational Effectiveness is arguably its ability to release value from the business and return it to members through better rates and flexible products. A key determinant of this measure is the society's average cost per transaction. This continues to fall, declining from £1.56 to £1.46 from 2001 to 2002. The continuous improvements to processes that impact upon customer value, satisfaction and retention are reflected in this impressive measure. Above all, the response of members confirms that Nationwide is doing the right things, and doing them well. When asked 'are we easy to do business with?', 87.2 per cent answer with either 'excellent' or 'very good'.

Engaging people

Shifting to the dimension of *engaging people*, we find Nationwide is an organisation that puts people at the heart of the business.

Nationwide recognises that delivering member value begins with happy, knowledgeable and committed employees. An extraordinary commitment to staff happiness leads to the society's goal of being a 'no vacancies' employer. Nationwide intends to achieve this state through a combination of very low turnover and a waiting list of potential employees. Nationwide staff are genuinely proud of the society and do not hide their loyalty. The society aspires to a top 10 place in the annual *Sunday Times* 'Best Places to Work' report – it is currently 'bubbling under' the top 20.

Nationwide's employee opinion census has been running since 1993. Results from the survey are analysed, correlated with customer service and business performance data, and then communicated and enacted at group, divisional, departmental and team level. The society also runs more than 20 incentive schemes, including employee of the month and year, and individual and team bonuses. These schemes distribute around £30 million per year to employees.

The recruitment process is geared towards hiring talented people who naturally display the behaviours needed to deliver Nationwide's service proposition and business results. Behavioural attributes and preferences are balanced with the knowledge and skills necessary to perform individual roles within the business.

Nationwide reviews its people needs every quarter. The review takes in both raw numbers of staff required and the skill and knowledge profile required to deliver the society's products and services. The resource plan is mapped to departmental level and identifies the actions needed to fill any identified gaps. Every role in the business has an associated development plan. In addition, each specialist and managerial role has an identified successor, ensuring that the society has future visibility of key personnel.

Employee performance agreements contain development plans including objectives for gaining or consolidating skills, knowledge and behaviours essential to the role. Competency-based development frameworks and assessment processes are used to manage performance, and all plans are reviewed half-yearly.

Leadership and values

The dimension of *leadership and values* is another conspicuous factor in Nationwide's success. Indeed, the society extends its leadership to its sector via the promotion of its values throughout the industry.

Leadership begins at the grass roots level with a programme of regular Talkback events where members can engage with the directors. Talkback events are held around the country, and increasingly over the net. A video on PRIDE helps to convey the society's values to new employees and make those values live. The acronym stands for **P**utting members first, **R**ising to the challenge, **I**nspiring confidence, **D**elivering best value and **E**xceeding expectations. The society's plain-dealing values are evident in employee services such as its free counselling service. The same values extend to member services: most accounts can be opened with £1, so that no potential customer need feel excluded.

All Nationwide managers are trained to recognise positive employee behaviours and the application of the society's values. Being alert to these attributes of staff performance is given equal weight with business goals. There is no sense that the society's values are a cosmetic ingredient of the business, to be dropped hastily in a crisis. Managers are empowered to recognise and reward behaviours through in-house schemes such as Service Heroes and Excellence in Action.

The society also has a stepped leadership development programme to ensure that its values persist through the forward planning of the business. The programme is designed to build leadership behaviours, knowledge and skills in the whole management team, from junior to senior levels. Individuals demonstrating high potential are assessed and then undertake a tailored development programme including individual coaching, mentoring and learning.

Nationwide's contribution to the community is extensive. Well known for its sponsorship of the England football team, the society also supports football at lower levels through local schools and clubs. In October 2001, Nationwide distributed 6 million reflectors – one for every primary schoolchild in the UK.

This kind of thoughtful, neighbourhood-level approach scales naturally to Nationwide's interventions at the industry level. Its firm stance against transaction charges at cash machines stopped charges becoming commonplace in the British market. More recently, its decision to show comparisons of credit card charges in an 'honesty box' on literature influenced the Treasury committee on credit cards. As a result, since April 2004 all credit card providers have been obliged to follow suit. While Hughes is proud that Nationwide is 'fighting for transparent, honest values', he makes it clear that the goal is not exactly altruism: 'transparency makes us more competitive and shows customers just what a good deal they can get at Nationwide.' Nationwide's values are human, but they are commercial too.

Organisational agility

Examples of *organisational agility* abound at Nationwide, and all are instructive. As a mass-market player in an intensely competitive but closely regulated industry, Nationwide must be able to respond confidently and competently to events in double-quick time. One example is the issue of Dual Mortgage Pricing. The industry's ombudsman disagreed with the way the society (and its competitors) wanted to reward the loyalty of existing borrowers. The ruling arrived on 7 February, triggering a decision whether to fight the ruling or adjust the accounts of over 400,000 members who were affected. Nationwide announced its decision to abide by the ombudsman's decision on 21 February, while its competitors decided to fight the ruling. The practical consequences included taking the decision-making process through to board approval, and communicating the account adjustment plan to the entire staff. The society had to solve the technical problem of adjusting a mountain of accounts which would have taken the entire staff 20 years to accomplish, working 24 hours per day – if they did it manually. The team also had to develop processes to address queries and one-off account exceptions, while telling the affected borrowers what was happening. The member communication was sent on 7 March – just 1 month after the initial trigger. The project went live on 21 March: an extraordinary response to an extraordinary demand.

Organisational agility also comes into play when Nationwide initiates its own business changes. The TakeAway remortgage product is a prime example. Research showed potential mortgage customers understood the savings they could make by moving their mortgage to Nationwide but did not necessarily want to undergo the full application process, especially the standard mortgage interview. In July 2001 the society had the idea of offering a 'TakeAway mortgage' – in a bag. The bag's contents let customers drive the process themselves. It also allows them to engage with the society without spending much time in the branch. Considering their new mortgage can become something that customers do in the natural setting of their own home.

The concept immediately generated a list of challenges to solve. What would be the legal implications of customers using a self-service approach? What systems would be needed to handle the completed applications? What additional training did retail staff need to support the pack? Could the society design a practical and attractive package and produce it in-house to budget and on time? And what were the cultural implications of the new product: would customer advisors regard it as a threat to their role?

Dedication, cooperation and imagination saw the TakeAway launched on time in just 3 months. Nationwide's share of the remortgage market has grown more than tenfold since that time, a success largely attributed to the novel finance-in-a-bag idea and its rapid delivery.

Is Nationwide at the end of its service excellence journey? No one at Nationwide believes the organisation has reached a peak in service excellence and can afford to rest on its laurels. 'We are not complacent,' says Hughes, stressing that Nationwide is continuing to work through the PRIDE programme internally and continuing to benchmark the society against other organisations in a wide variety of sectors at home and abroad. The development of the business continues to major on streamlining processes, taking costs out of the business to return value to members, and fighting for customers' best interests.

Tim Hughes's advice to other organisations pursuing service excellence shares the openness and practicality the society has brought to all the activities explored in the Awards process. Hughes says first of all that service excellence must not be seen as an abstract concept, but related strongly to real business drivers. He believes that linking service excellence practices to business goals such as repurchase and retention generates more excitement within the team, and greater clarity of purpose. His final piece of advice is to 'focus on your people. They deliver the service, and they are the brand'.

Benchmark your practices

Our aims with this book have been to:

- guide organisations to future success by helping them to understand what key ingredients of service excellence are;
- help organisations develop in ways that they can be proud of and that will provide them with sustainable competitive advantage for the future.

We can point to research that suggests that learning by sharing best practice and then building on what works in your organisation means you will start to do less of what does not work. This is known as 'appreciative inquiry' and simply adopting this as a part of how you do your business, whatever that business may be, will work to improve the levels of service you deliver to your customers. Our hope is that in sharing the insights into service excellence that we have gained as judges and in the telling of the stories behind the Awards winners, we may inspire you to greater things.

If reading these success stories makes you wonder how well your organisation would compare, then why not benchmark yourself by taking part in the Unisys/Management Today Service Excellence Awards? Every entrant receives a tailored diagnosis so that they can assess their own approach to service excellence against that of their peers and the best in the UK. Individually produced for each organisation, your benchmark report will provide valuable improvement-oriented feedback, and will offer more insight into how leading companies are tackling today's key issues. Full details are given at www.serviceexcellenceawards.com

Concluding remarks

We are proud to have been associated with the Unisys/Management Today Service Excellence Awards programme over a number of years as judges and pleased to have been able to share our learning through this book. Feedback from readers is welcomed and should be directed to m.k.clark@cranfield.ac.uk or s.l.baker@cranfield. ac.uk.

2003 Service Excellence Awards

Self-assessment questionnaire

This is a reproduction of the contents of the 2003 Management Today/ Unisys Service Excellence Awards, self-assessment questionnaire.

Please complete the following information about yourself:

Submission contact:		
0.1	Name:	
	E-mail address:	
	Telephone number:	
	Job title:	

Who is the person sponsoring – providing commitment, time and resource.

Submission sponsor:		
0.2	Name:	
	E-mail address:	
	Telephone number:	
	Job title:	

Please provide the following organisation details, and then select your preferred Award category:

Organisation details:		
0.3	Organisation name:	
	Organisation address:	

0.4	**Please select a Service Excellence Award category:** (mark 'X' once only)	
Business to Business – includes logistics and business services		
Retail and Consumer Services – includes travel and utilities		
Financial Services – includes banks, building societies, insurance and investment services		
Manufacturing/Engineering – includes construction and process industries		
Public Services – includes government, education and not-for-profit organisations		

Please provide the following supplementary organisation details (space is provided for comments and explanations):

Supplementary organisation details:			
0.5	Number of people employed in the organisation (full time equivalent staff):	Covered by the submission	The whole organisation
Your comments:			
0.6	Net sales or operating budget for the past 5 years (current year is your last full financial year):		

Current year	Year-1	Year-2	Year-3	Year-4

Your comments:

0.7	Net profit or operating surplus for the past 5 years (current year is your last full financial year):			
Current year	Year-1	Year-2	Year-3	Year-4

Your comments:

0.8	Number of sites (offices, retail outlets, branches, factories, etc.)	Covered by the submission	The whole organisation

Your comments:

0.9	Which of the following standards/systems do you actively use to improve your business		
ISO 9000/2000	Investors in People	Charter Mark	EFQM

Your comments:

In no more than 500 words, please describe the nature and scope of your business activities.

(*Note*: only the first 500 words will be taken into account.)

1. Customer intelligence

This vector of the assessment addresses how you build an understanding of the needs and expectations of your customers, and how they perceive your performance.

Please mark a box in the 'your response' column against the line that best describes the degree to which your organisation reflects the following statements. You should be confident in your ability to support your answer with documentary evidence when requested. The Judges will mark down unsubstantiated responses. **Please limit your supporting comments to no more than 50 words.**

Space is provided at the end of each section for additional written evidence in support of your entry.

1.1	**We encourage and act on feedback from customers:**	**Your response** (mark 'X' once)
✪	We do not actively elicit feedback from customers	
✪	↕ *between* ↕	
✪	We periodically research customer needs	
✪	↕ *between* ↕	
✪	Collecting and acting on customer and market data is part of our culture and systems	

Statement notes
How effective is your organisation at collecting feedback from customers and then using it to drive changes to products, services and ways of doing business?

Your comments:

1.2	**We understand the drivers of customer satisfaction:**	**Your response** (mark 'X' once)
✪	We rely on intuition to tell us what customers want	
✪	↕ *between* ↕	
✪	We have wide and deep understanding of our chosen customers	
✪	↕ *between* ↕	
✪	We research our customers' customers and the wider socio-economic environment	

Statement notes
How well does your organisation understand the factors that motivate customers to buy?

Your comments:

1.3	**We are recognised as innovators in our market:**	**Your response** (mark 'X' once)
✪	We can show a link between innovation and improved customer satisfaction and sales	
✪	⇕ *between* ⇕	
✪	Customers recognise us for delivering innovations that improve customer service	
✪	⇕ *between* ⇕	
✪	Customers perceive us as late adopters of service innovations	

Statement notes
Does your organisation lead the market in developing new products/services and ways of doing business, or is it always lagging what competitors and new entrants do?

Your comments:

1.4	**We build long-term, profitable relationships in our chosen markets:**	**Your response** (mark 'X' once)
✪	Any customer is a good customer	
✪	⇕ *between* ⇕	
✪	We work only in carefully defined market segments	
✪	⇕ *between* ⇕	
✪	Customer value data is used to target relationships in defined market segments	

Statement notes
Has your organisation carefully segmented the market? Does it track the profitability of chosen customers and use this information to refine relationship management?

Your comments:

1.5	**We monitor and track customer retention and repurchase intention:**	**Your response** (mark 'X' once)
✪	We cannot track individual customer retention or repurchase intention	
✪	↕ *between* ↕	
✪	We can identify retention and repurchase intention of all customers	
✪	↕ *between* ↕	
✪	We can predict retention and repurchase intention and their financial impact	

Statement notes
Does your organisation track and analyse the purchase patterns of individual customers in order to provide information to improve repurchase intention and retention?

Your comments:

Please complete the customer intelligence supporting data questions below:

> > > > > > > > > Customer intelligence < < < < < < < < <		
1.6 How many customers do you serve?	Total	Active

Total customers are the number of customers your organisation maintains records for. This applies to both internal and external customers. Active customer – someone who has purchased products/services in the last 2 years.
Public sector organisations – number of people that have used your products/services. This can also apply to internal customers.

Your comments:

1.7	What percentages of customers express themselves as:			

☺ Delighted	Satisfied	☺ Neutral	Dissatisfied	☹ Very dissatisfied

If you use different categorisations for customer satisfaction, please convert to the above groupings. Only include figures that you can support with data.

Your comments:

1.8	How many pieces of formal customer feedback does your organisation receive each year?				
Surveys	Complaints	Compliments	Focus groups	Others (give details)	

A survey returned or attendance at a focus group counts as one piece.

Your comments:

1.9	Please tell us the percentages of active customers that:

(a) Make a repeat purchase	(b) Recommend your products/services to others

Repeat purchase refers to a customer that buys the same product/service more than once in 2 years or who buys additional products/services. When quoting a figure, please ensure that you can support that with documentary evidence. If you have no data to support it, do not enter a figure.

Your comments:

1.10	How frequently is customer satisfaction data analysed and communicated?				
Weekly	Monthly	Quarterly	Annually	Bi-annually

The frequency at which data is formally analysed, presented and communicated to key managers and teams in the organisation.

Your comments:

In 500 words or less, please provide details of things you do that you consider being examples of 'customer intelligence' best practice.

2. Operational effectiveness

2003

This vector of the assessment addresses how effective your service delivery programmes and processes are, and how easy your organisation is to do business with.

Please mark a box in the 'your response' column against the line that best describes the degree to which your organisation reflects the following statements. You should be confident in your ability to support your answer with documentary evidence when requested. The Judges will mark down unsubstantiated responses. **Please limit your supporting comments to no more than 50 words.**

Space is provided at the end of each section for additional written evidence in support of your entry.

2.1	Customers consider us easy to do business with:	Your response (mark 'X' once)
✪	Feedback shows that our business processes and systems are not customer friendly	
✪	⇕ *between* ⇕	
✪	Customers commend us on the ease and efficiency of business systems and processes	
✪	⇕ *between* ⇕	
✪	We can charge a premium price because of the quality of the customer experience	

Statement notes
Being easy to do business with refers to access to information, simplicity and friendliness of systems and procedures and the willingness of your organisation to make life easy for customers.

Your comments:

2.2	We enhance business performance through continuous improvement (CI):	Your response (mark 'X' once)
✪	Organisation wide, data driven CI leads to improved business results	
✪	⇕ *between* ⇕	
✪	CI is a regular, organisation wide activity	
✪	⇕ *between* ⇕	
✪	Performance improvement is an ad-hoc activity	

Statement notes
Promoting continuous improvement is the environment that managers create to encourage people to identify and improve the product/service delivery chain.

Your comments:

2.3	We can deal equally effectively with customers over multiple channels:	Your response (mark 'X' once)
✪	Sales and service channels are independent of each other	
✪	↕ *between* ↕	
✪	Sales and service channels are partially integrated	
✪	↕ *between* ↕	
✪	Customers experience the same, high level of service across all channels	

Statement notes
How well has your organisation integrated its different delivery channels, allowing the customer to chose or switch channels and still receive the same level of service?

Your comments:

2.4	We deal with service failures effectively:	Your response (mark 'X' once)
✪	Service recovery turns customers into advocates and generates service improvements	
✪	↕ *between* ↕	
✪	Failures are corrected to the customer's satisfaction and improvements actioned	
✪	↕ *between* ↕	
✪	We correct service failures when they occur	

Statement notes
Service recovery refers to the speed and effectiveness with which your organisation responds to a failure to deliver the required service or a dissatisfied customer.

Your comments:

2.5	**We use the web to enhance the customer's experience:**	**Your response** (mark 'X' once)
✪	We use the web to provide information of value to the customer	
✪	↕ *between* ↕	
✪	Web-based transactions improve service and reduce transaction costs	
✪	↕ *between* ↕	
✪	We use the web to build profitable relationships based on information freely shared	

Statement notes
Does your organisation use the World Wide Web to enhancing the experience for customers by providing information and transactional facilities?

Your comments:

Please complete the operational effectiveness supporting data questions below:

> > > > > > > > > **Operational effectiveness** < < < < < < < < <			
2.6	What is the percentage of your transactions that are error free?		

An error-free customer transaction is where a customer orders, receives and pays for a product/ service and no errors are made across the transaction chain.

Your comments:

2.7	Which of the following techniques are used to improve operational effectiveness?		
Six Sigma	Statistical process control	Benchmarking	Other (give details)

You should tick the box ONLY if the technique is used widely across your organisation, and has formal tools and methods to support its implementation.

Your comments:

2.8	If you ticked benchmarking, which of the following do you practice?		
		Numerical	Process benchmarking
	Internal		
	Industry		
	X-industry		

Numerical benchmarking: benchmarking of quantifiable factors; e.g. customer satisfaction, financial performance, cycle time. Process benchmarking: comparison of the techniques and methods that drive performance. Internal: Comparison of performance with different divisions/ teams/geographies within your organisation. Industry: comparison of performance with other organisations in your industry or sector. Cross industry: comparison of performance with other organisations across all industries and market sectors. You should tick the box ONLY if the technique is used widely across your organisation and has formal tools and methods to support its implementation.

Your comments:

2.9	Do you track the cost per transaction? If yes, please state the average cost:		
Yes	No	Current financial year	Previous financial year

Transaction costs are the cost of servicing a single transaction. Examples include the cost of processing a membership request, the cost of selling a product or the cost of completing an insurance claim. The question asks for the average cost of all transactions.

Your comments:

2.10	Do you track the cost of non-conformance? If yes, please state the total cost:		
Yes	No	Current financial year	Previous financial year

The costs of non-conformance are those costs associated with failure to do things right first time. These would include costs of re-work, scrap, administering complaints and any discounts or refunds given to customers.

Your comments:

In 500 words or less, please provide details of things you do that you consider being examples of 'operational effectiveness' best practice.

3. Engaging people

2003

This vector of the assessment addresses how well you have inspired the hearts and minds of people up and down your organisation to deliver great service.

Please mark a box in the 'your response' column against the line that best describes the degree to which your organisation reflects the following statements. You should be confident in your ability to support your answer with documentary evidence when requested. The Judges will mark down unsubstantiated responses. **Please limit your supporting comments to no more than 50 words.**

Space is provided at the end of each section for additional written evidence in support of your entry.

3.1	People have the right skills and knowledge to perform their work well:	Your response (mark 'X' once)
✪	Most people have most of the skills and knowledge they need to perform their work well	
✪	↕ *between* ↕	
✪	All our people have the skills and knowledge they need to perform their work well	
✪	↕ *between* ↕	
✪	Multi-skilling enables people to work well in more than one role	

Statement notes
To what extent do your people have the skills and knowledge needed work effectively across the organisation.

Your comments:

3.2	**We regularly monitor people satisfaction and act on the findings:**	**Your response** (mark 'X' once)
✪	We can demonstrate business benefit from improving people satisfaction	
✪	⇕ *between* ⇕	
✪	An ongoing programme of measuring people satisfaction drives clear actions	
✪	⇕ *between* ⇕	
✪	People satisfaction is systematically measured annually	

Statement notes
Regular monitoring is exemplified by periodic surveys that are followed up by actions and performance improvements that are attributed to the results of the surveys.

Your comments:

3.3	**We recognise the performance and behaviour of outstanding individuals and teams:**	**Your response** (mark 'X' once)
✪	We have an effective and widely used recognition scheme	
✪	⇕ *between* ⇕	
✪	Through formal and informal recognition we regularly acknowledge great performance	
✪	⇕ *between* ⇕	
✪	Imaginative and widespread recognition leads to improved motivation and performance	

Statement notes
The degree to which your organisation formally and informally recognises and praises instances of good performance.

Your comments:

3.4	**We empower people to deliver service excellence:**	**Your response** (mark 'X' once)
✪	When dealing with customers, people can act within carefully defined limits	
✪	⥮ *between* ⥮	
✪	We encourage people to use initiative and judgement when dealing with customers	
✪	⥮ *between* ⥮	
✪	Customer feedback proves that people are empowered to deliver service excellence	

Statement notes
To what extent does your organisation give people the responsibility and the authority to do what is needed to satisfy customers?

Your comments:

3.5	**When recruiting and developing people we focus on attitudes first:**	**Your response** (mark 'X' once)
✪	People with the wrong attitudes are actively managed out, however they perform	
✪	⥮ *between* ⥮	
✪	Attitudes are the primary determinant of recruitment, reward and promotion	
✪	⥮ *between* ⥮	
✪	Attitude is an important factor in recruitment, reward and promotion of people	

Statement notes
The extent to which your organisation implements its values through the training, development and growth of its people.

Your comments:

Please complete the engaging people supporting data questions below:

> > > > > > > > > **Engaging people** < < < < < < < < <

3.6	What was your total spend on training and development last year?	

The total direct costs of training and development including the costs of any external courses and conferences that were funded out of the training budget.

Your comments:

3.7	How many formal recognition awards were given last year?	

Formal recognitions include those that carry a reward and written recognitions, and may be issued by managers, peers or customers.

Your comments:

3.8	What percentages of your people express themselves as:

☺ Very satisfied	Satisfied	☹ Neutral	Dissatisfied	☹ Very dissatisfied

If you use different categorisations for employee satisfaction, please convert to the above groupings. Only include figures that you can support with data.

Your comments:

3.9	What percentages of your people are actively engaged in the following practices?

	Managers %	Entire workforce %
Performance appraisal		
360 degree appraisal		
Personal development plans		
Suggestion schemes		
Recognition schemes		
Succession planning		

Your comments:

3.10	How many working days were lost through absenteeism last year?	

Quote the total number of working days lost due to sickness and unauthorised absence.

Your comments:

In 500 words or less, please provide details of things you do that you consider being examples of 'engaging people' best practice.

4. Leadership and values

2003

This vector of the assessment addresses the direction and culture of the organisation, and how successfully your values and leadership create a passion for customers.

Please mark a box in the 'your response' column against the line that best describes the degree to which your organisation reflects the following statements. You should be confident in your ability to support your answer with documentary evidence when requested. The Judges will mark down unsubstantiated responses. **Please limit your supporting comments to no more than 50 words.**

Space is provided at the end of each section for additional written evidence in support of your entry.

4.1	**Our values are widely understood and practised:**	**Your response** (mark 'X' once)
✪	People understand the implications of our values	
✪	⇕ *between* ⇕	
✪	The majority of people can articulate how the values underpin what they do	
✪	⇕ *between* ⇕	
✪	We can demonstrate how people refer to the organisation's values in their work	
Statement notes *To what extent do people across your organisation understand the values and reflect this understanding in their daily work and behaviour?*		
Your comments:		

4.2	**Leadership reflects the organisation's values:**	**Your response** (mark 'X' once)
✪	Leadership actions and values are often contradictory	
✪	⇕ *between* ⇕	
✪	Values are visible in our leadership	
✪	⇕ *between* ⇕	
✪	Values are central; managers who ignore them are managed out of the organisation	
Statement notes *The degree to which leaders act in accordance with your organisation's stated values.*		
Your comments:		

4.3	**Our processes of management enact our values:**	**Your response** (mark 'X' once)
✪	We can show how values are actively reinforced through management processes	
✪	⇕ *between* ⇕	
✪	Some management systems reflect the organisation's values	
✪	⇕ *between* ⇕	
✪	There is little relationship *between* our values and how this organisation is managed	

Statement notes
The degree to which the processes such as communication, recognition, reward, recruitment, change and measurement reinforce your organisation's stated values.

Your comments:

4.4	**Senior managers actively champion customers:**	**Your response** (mark 'X' once)
✪	Senior managers spend little time with customers	
✪	⇕ *between* ⇕	
✪	Senior managers always consider the customer in their decisions and actions	
✪	⇕ *between* ⇕	
✪	Senior managers purposefully design a customer-centric organisation	

Statement notes
To what degree are senior managers seen to champion the cause of customers in your organisation?

Your comments:

4.5	We invest in developing leadership across the organisation:	Your response (mark 'X' once)
✪	Leadership development is targeted only at managers	
✪	↕ *between* ↕	
✪	Leadership training is available for people at all levels of the organisation	
✪	↕ *between* ↕	
✪	We systematically identify and develop leadership across the organisation	

Statement notes
To what extent does your organisation seek to develop its leadership capability at all parts and all levels of the organisation?

Your comments:

Please complete the leadership and values supporting data questions below:

> > > > > > > > >   Leadership and Values   < < < < < < < < <

4.6	What is the percentage of your people that have undertaken formal leadership training?	

The percentage of the total number of people in your organisation who have undertaken some leadership training in the past three years.

Your comments:

4.7	How many days of leadership training were provided last year?	

The total number of man-days of leadership training delivered. This figure should refer to focused leadership training only. Do not include training in basic management skills.

Your comments:

4.8	What percentages of your current top team joined the organisation as:

Front line worker	Supervisor/ team leader	Middle manager	Senior manager	Hired to top team

The top team is the most senior level executive management team in your organisation.

Your comments:

4.9	Do you have a formal statement of organisational values?	Yes	
		No	

Organisational values may be called beliefs or principles.

Your comments:

4.10	If you answered 'Yes' to Q4.9, please tick all of the following that are covered:				
People	Customers	Continuous improvement	Environment	Performance
Society/ community	Integrity	Fun	Learning	Innovation

Only tick the item if your values statement explicitly includes that item.

Your comments:

In 500 words or less, please provide details of things you do that you consider being examples of 'leadership and values' best practice.

5.   Organisational agility

2003

This vector of the assessment addresses how well your organisation anticipates and responds to the changing world.

Please mark a box in the 'your response' column against the line that best describes the degree to which your organisation reflects the following statements. You should be confident in your ability to support your answer with documentary evidence when requested. The Judges will mark down unsubstantiated responses. **Please limit your supporting comments to no more than 50 words.**

Space is provided at the end of each section for additional written evidence in support of your entry.

5.1	**Constructive criticism is an essential element of our culture:**	**Your response** (mark 'X' once)
✪	People will offer constructive criticism selectively	
✪	⇕ *between* ⇕	
✪	Constructive criticism is offered widely without fear of retribution	
✪	⇕ *between* ⇕	
✪	Leadership and processes encourage constructive criticism which is taken seriously	

Statement notes
To what extent does your organisation allow people to challenge the decisions and plans of their managers?

Your comments:

5.2	**The organisation provides methods, tools and training to enable change:**	**Your response** (mark 'X' once)
✪	A comprehensive suite of tools and methods help to deliver successful changes	
✪	⇕ *between* ⇕	
✪	A comprehensive range of effective change tools are widely used	
✪	⇕ *between* ⇕	
✪	Limited methods, tools and training are used in parts of the organisation	

Statement notes
To what extent do you invest in equipping people across your organisation to manage change?

Your comments:

5.3	**We have tools and techniques that facilitate the capture and sharing of knowledge and expertise:**	**Your response** (mark 'X' once)
✪	Tools and techniques for KM are used by some parts of the organisation	
✪	↕ *between* ↕	
✪	We have effective tools and techniques for KM that are widely used	
✪	↕ *between* ↕	
✪	We can show how our culture of KM generates significant performance improvements	

Statement notes
To what extent is the sharing of knowledge and expertise supported and facilitated across your organisation? We use KM to abbreviate the phrase 'facilitate the sharing of knowledge and expertise across the organisation'.

Your comments:

5.4	**The organisation monitors and shares information about the changing socio-economic environment:**	**Your response** (mark 'X' once)
✪	Organisation wide systems for environmental scanning link to decision making	
✪	↕ *between* ↕	
✪	Information is collected and readily available across the organisation	
✪	↕ *between* ↕	
✪	Information is gathered but not widely shared	

Statement notes
How well does your organisation understand the socio-economic and political changes in the environment(s) in which it has to function?

Your comments:

5.5	**Our people respond positively to change:**	**Your response** (mark 'X' once)
✪	Change is viewed with concern	
✪	⇕ *between* ⇕	
✪	People are supportive of change	
✪	⇕ *between* ⇕	
✪	Feedback and actions show that people embrace change as natural and essential	

Statement notes
How do people react in your organisation when faced with change?

Your comments:

Please complete the organisational agility supporting data questions below:

> > > > > > > > > **Organisational agility** < < < < < < < < <

5.6	For which of the following does your organisation have a formal monitoring programme?

Competitors	Customer's customers	Social trends	Economic trends

Only tick the box if your organisation can show that it has established formal approaches to monitoring that aspect of the external environment.

Your comments:

5.7	With reference to managing change, which of the following are in place across your organisation?

Common approach or methodology	Common tools	Change management training programmes	Forum(s) for sharing experiences and best practices	Post project/ activity reviews

Only tick the box if your organisation can show that it has established systematic approaches to that aspect of the question.

Your comments:

| **5.8** | What is the percentage of your people that have undertaken formal training in managing change? | |

The percentage of the total number of people in your organisation that have undertaken some change management training in the past 3 years.

Your comments:

| **5.9** | How many days of change management training were provided last year? | |

The total number of man-days of change management training delivered. This figure should refer to focused change management training only. Do not include training in basic management skills.

Your comments:

| **5.10** | List the performance indicators that are used to manage the business at the highest level? |

List the performance indicators (e.g. profit, revenue, customer satisfaction) that are used by the most senior management team to monitor the performance of your organisation. Only include those items that are regularly reported, reviewed and acted upon.

Your response:

In 500 words or less, please provide details of things you do that you consider being examples of 'organisational agility' best practice.

Index